Fame™

D0358978

£2.50

CONTENTS

STORIES

FEATURES

Copyright © MCMLXXXII
by Metro-Goldwyn-Mayer Inc.
All rights reserved throughout the world.
Published in Great Britain by
World International Publishing Limited.
A Pentos Company,
P. O. Box 111, Great Ducie Street, Manchester M60 3BL.
Printed in Belgium.
SBN 7235 6676 3.

ABOUT THE SHOW

Set against the backdrop of New York's famous stage school, The School of The Arts, *Fame* explores the dreams and challenges of the students there, who each has his or her own particular longing to achieve that elusive quality: fame.

Originally a hugely-successful feature film, the idea has now been brought to the small screen, whilst remaining true to the high-energy excitement of the movie version.

MGM describe the series as 'an adventure in entertainment for audiences of all ages'. Shot entirely on location in New York, it introduces a platoon of talented new stars in the key roles, and both collectively and individually they bring the shows to life, playing out all the stories

Another one for the album.

**Some of the stars of *Fame* line up for a happy shot, taken during a photo session in a break from rehearsals. They are, from left to right...
Top Row: Lee Curreri, Carol Mayo Jenkins and Albert Hague. Middle Row: P.R. Paul, Valerie Landsburg and Debbie Allen. Bottom Row: Lori Singer, Gene Anthony Ray, Carlo Imperato and Erica Gimpel.**

which encompass the dreams and the hopes, the tragedies and the triumphs of the school.

Executive producer Jerry Isenberg likened the early days of the production to something from the golden era of Hollywood, when mighty studios such as MGM regularly sent out their scouts to discover and groom new talent for future stardom. The producers of *Fame* went into schools, and held auditions all over America before finally casting the actors and actresses for the show. It wasn't that there was a shortage of talent—quite the reverse in fact—but the producers wanted the best.

And they certainly found just that!

One Small Step

The snow lay round about, deep and crisp and even. A wintry blanket of white had descended over the city, making it look clean, untouched, perfect. Telegraph wires hung like white ropes from the poles, the lines of cars resembled a production line of giant iced cakes, and the trees bowed down, their branches filled with snowy blossom.

If the sudden invasion of the snow slowed the world down a little, the world did not mind too much. It bound people together in a strange way as they battled the elements, sharing stories of abandoned cars and disorganised days, the inadequacy of the city works department, and the inaccuracy of the weathermen. Brothers in adversity, they shared the childish joy of normality suspended and the world transformed. Snowflakes floated down, the city lay in a half-dream.

Outside the School of The Arts the snow was falling in considerable quantity, in fist-size balls whose flights criss-crossed the front of the building and exploded on body, brick and sidewalk in a ceaseless spray of white.

Coco gathered up a handful of snow, moulded it with her gloves, ducked a passing missile, and let fly with her own. Lydia Grant's right shoulder spun back as the snowball crashed against her and splintered into crystal fragments.

It took Coco a fraction of a second to duck down behind a cluster of boys and emerge from the other side, bag hung demurely by her side, an innocent passer by like Lydia.

One or two other members of staff had also fallen victim to the crossfire, and with Lydia's help the chaotic battleground returned to peace.

"You could have somebody's eye out with a weapon like that, honey!" said Lydia sternly, disarming a student before moving on to break up other nearby ranks.

She shook the snow from her collar, shivered as a number of particles escaped inside her clothes, melting cold into her skin. Elizabeth Sherwood came along the street, tightly wrapped inward, head bowed against the falling snow.

"Hi, Lydia," she said with surprise, almost walking into her colleague. "Glad to see the ceasefire was called before I arrived. I see you took a direct hit."

She helped Lydia fluff out the tiara of snowflakes that sparkled in her hair like diamonds. Lydia drew herself up, pulled her collar in, and the two of them trudged over to the entrance.

"Is it just because we grow up," asked Lydia as they walked, "that snowstorms become a bad thing, or have they always been a bad thing, and we were just too dumb to know any better when we were kids?"

Elizabeth Sherwood laughed, linking her arm with Lydia as they mounted the well-ploughed steps to the entrance. "It's nothing to do with the weather," she answered. "If it's summer it's too hot—it's the same thing. Being grown up is what causes it. They ought to pass a law against becoming adult, it spoils all the fun."

"I feel old," complained Doris, looking out of the window at the white ribbon of roadway below, the furrows of car tracks like railway lines on the blank surface. "Maybe it's the weather. It all looks so bright and new, and I feel like yesterday's leftovers. Maybe I've missed my chance and passed my peak; I should have been a child star. What do you think?"

"About you being old, or the weather?" asked Montgomery, pressing his face against the glass.

"Let's stick to the weather, okay?" suggested Doris. "I think I'll like it better that way."

"Ouch! That's cold," cried Montgomery, stepping back from the window, a burning glow on his face.

"I feel slowed down," said Julie, rubbing her arms briskly to stir her circulation. "Everything feels that bit harder to do when you're cold, you move that bit more slowly."

Danny joined the group surveying the scene below.

"You can warm yourself up on Friday."

"How's that?"

"Bruno's holding a party over at his place."

"Bruno? Holding a party?" asked Montgomery, gathering up his belongings.

"Did you hear that?" asked Danny as the group began to drift off along the corridor heading for class. "This guy should try putting a memory act together. What recall!"

Montgomery aimed a blow and missed.

"Oh yeah," remembered Danny, "and if anybody's interested, a little cabaret is being put together. Quality acts only, of course, no riff-raff."

"That lets you out then," observed Montgomery.

"Lets me out nothing!" retorted Danny. "I'm the one who's bringing the show a touch of class. Your Master of Ceremonies for the evening, direct from New York—"

"—this is New York—"

"—direct from New York, that talented young comedian… need I say more?" enquired Danny nonchalantly.

Doris looked at him with amazement. "Bruno chose you as comedian for the night?"

Danny rankled slightly. "Yeah, me. Why not? Who else would he pick?"

"Attila the Hun, maybe?"

Coco Hernandez enjoyed being at the School of The Arts. She wasn't mad about studying, the reading and writing side of school, but it wasn't awful. She understood that it was important to gain a regular education and she was a bright enough student not to make heavy weather of it. She did what was required of her, and if she didn't pour her enthusiasm completely into the academic side of things it was because she had other interests that claimed priority.

She knew she was good. She had a great future as a dancer, as a singer, she had no doubts as to what direction she was headed in. So while she did put in the work to maintain her grades in the regular subjects, she reserved her main energies for what she felt was truly important to her future.

For the millionth time she

reflected on her good fortune in finding a place at the School of The Arts where she could develop her talents, hone them to the degree of professionalism she knew was necessary for her to make it in her chosen career.

At the same time she was aware it was not simply good fortune that had landed her in this place. It was talent. She was acutely aware of how good she actually was, and if she sometimes struck other students as having a high opinion of herself it was because it was justified.

It was true that she was less arrogant about her talent than she had been when she was younger, for as she and her abilities had matured under the sure hands of her teachers two things had slowly dawned on her. The first was how much she still had to learn; that had been a hard lesson to grasp,

and even now she was too young to fully comprehend that nothing can replace actual experience. Nevertheless, the more she found herself developing under people like Lydia the more her respect for her teachers' skills, the result of years of application and hard work, grew.

The second realisation that she had found creeping into her consciousness was that real talent did not have to draw attention continually to itself. If at one time she had been an inveterate exhibitionist, showing off at the slightest opportunity, thrusting her superiority into other people's faces all the time, she had now begun to allow her talent to speak for itself.

She was still undeniably extrovert, taking any chance she could to display her abilities, but as she'd grown up the reasons for it had subtly changed. It was more

the case now that she danced and sang 'in public' because of the sheer enjoyment it gave her to do so. She was in love with what she did for its own sake and her desire to demonstrate it was uncontrollable. She was addicted to performing.

These changes in her attitude, the gradual move from childish bigheadedness to adult professionalism, had not, however, blunted her ambition or her sense of competitiveness. The will to succeed had been sharpened, focused more clearly, as her awareness of the professional world of entertainment had grown. And while the thrill of an audience's applause had remained as bright and brilliant as ever, her awareness of the need to improve, to expand her skills had concentrated her effort into a fierce and demanding process of dedicated and determined application to her music and dance lessons.

She was eager, even impatient, to be released into the big world, to put her talent to the test in the front line, and she strove perpetually to improve herself for the moment when the big break came, which she knew with adolescent certainty would come. Coco Hernandez was going to be a star, she sensed the inevitability of it, and every day brought it closer to reality. In the meantime, she put her heart and soul into preparing herself.

Ain't nothing going to stop me
Nothing stands in my way
I know just what I want
And I want it all today
Don't ask me if I doubt it
'Cos I won't hear you, man,
Only one place that I'm going
That fits in with my plan!

I'm going to the top (where?)
To the top of the tree
Never going to stop (when?)
Till that's reality!

I know I've got the talent
Baby that's for sure
And when I've made a million
Going to make me some more
Don't talk to me of failure
It's a word I don't know
Just point me at the future
And watch this girl go!

I'm going to the top (where?)
To the top of the tree
Never going to stop (when?)
Till that's reality!

Lydia Grant was as aware as Coco herself of the girl's potential. With Coco it was not so much encouragement that was needed as guidance. The energy which Coco poured into her work was like that of a space rocket engine thrusting powerfully against gravity, yearning to leap from the ground into the stratosphere. Lydia's job was to channel that relentless, immeasurable energy, make it work for Coco so that it was not dissipated and wasted.

She looked around the practice room. She was proud of her students. They worked hard, extraordinarily hard, and she understood the forces that drove them. But such talent and determination needed to be shaped, to be aimed at the right goals, to be disciplined by the necessities of the profession, refined until the raw energy of these young dancers was a polished and efficient expression of their capabilities, their imagination and flair.

Coco was learning fast, overtaking her teacher as she unstintingly progressed towards the stardom Lydia sensed would one day be hers. But as an older and wiser head, Lydia was also concerned

that Coco's temperament should match her dancing skills in development.

It was a hard, tough business she was entering and while Coco's singlemindedness impressed her teacher it was not enough to think only of ever growing success. Life was rarely like that, and Coco still had to learn to harness her determination to suceed to reality. It could, after all, be critical in how Coco coped with the uncertainties of a showbusiness career. She did not want to quench the girl's unquestionable spirit, but to broaden its awareness, prepare it for the real world.

Lydia brought her attention back to the class. Effort showed clearly on their faces, beads of perspiration mottled their features, like rain on a window pane. It had been a hard session. The exercise finished and the students relaxed on the floor.

"That's good," commented Lydia, positioning herself so that she faced the assembly. "That's the way to do it. Start slowly, don't push it too early. Gradually build up the pace without overdoing it.

She moved through the scattering of bodies, the deep breathing of

agile mover though he was, had no time to sidestep and the next moment he and Danny found themselves on the floor beneath a cascade of paper.

"Hey, man," complained Leroy, "you never heard of slowing down on bends? This Leroy's going to end up a write-off with crazies like you burning up the highway."

"Hey, sorry, Leroy," apologised Danny, scuffling round reassembling his file. "I guess my feet need a retread, I didn't see you in time."

Leroy grudgingly let it pass, and hauled himself up. Danny blocked his path, and picked up the last of the sheets.

"In fact, you're just the man I want to see," he said, shuffling the paper into a neat stack. "You heard about Bruno's party on Friday? I'm organising a little entertainment to give the evening a bit of class, and it just so happens I have a spot free, just begging for a top-line dance act to fill it. I though maybe you and Coco—"

Leroy's look stopped him dead.

"You're full of hot air, Amatullo, you know that?" asked Leroy, taking the answer as read. "Why can't you just ask a simple question, instead of hitting me with all this hype?"

Danny grinned sheepishly.

"Sure, Leroy. Do you and Coco want to do a number together in the show on Friday?"

"You hiring?"

"Just a little organising on the side," answered Danny. "I'm doing MC, so I'm putting a few acts together, asking round."

"I'm already booked. Coco too."

Danny's face dropped at the news, then his forehead wrinkled questioningly. "You and Coco are doing a show already? So where's the action?"

"Bruno's, musclehead," replied Leroy, deadpan. "I already been asked. I already said yeah." He anticipated Danny's question. "Coco too. Man, I hope you get yourself together by Friday or you're going to be US not MC."

Leroy smiled, smartly brought his hand up underneath Danny's

the students bearing witness to the effort they had put into the morning's work.

"Always remember," Lydia went on as she walked among them, "that your bodies can't just be switched on and off to this sort of thing. It's a living organism and it needs to be treated with care; you can't expect it to be still one moment and doing a hundred miles an hour the next."

The class murmured in amusement, acknowledging the accuracy of Lydia's metaphorical estimate of how hard their bodies had been pushed in the last exercise.

"It's especially important," said Lydia, continuing, coming to the back of the class and beginning to work her way forward again, "when the temperature's as low as it is today. However fit or supple you think your bodies are, when it's as cold as this your bones are more brittle, your muscles that much more sluggish. Don't drive them too hard too soon or something will give. Treat your body with respect, lead it gently in and build up gradually, give it time to loosen up." She halted and took in the whole class with a sweeping look. "All right. That's all for today. Class dismissed."

Danny rounded the corner of the corridor at speed, clutching a bundle of notes to his chest. Leroy, reassembled pile of papers, and disappeared round the corner as they exploded once more in the air in a shower of white.

Lydia nearly fell over his crouching figure as she turned into the corridor. She scowled at him as she looked up from his position on all fours.

"Try taking a little more care where you choose to practise your animal impressions, Mr. Amatullo," she said pointedly. "Some of us are getting a little old for emergency somersaults."

"Sorry, Miss Grant," said Danny, gathering his papers and standing up. "I'm kind of glad I ran into you—sorry, no pun intended. Has Bruno asked you to his party yet, this Friday coming? We're putting on a little entertainment to mark the occasion—"

"I heard," said Lydia, cutting him short. "I also heard that you're the evening's comic. But don't worry—I'm still coming."

Lydia moved off down the corridor, leaving Danny staring after her. "What am I?" he said to himself. "Telepathic all of a sudden?"

He didn't have any time to answer before Doris and Montgomery collided with him. The papers scattered across the corridor once more.

"Honestly," said Doris. "This guy will do anything for a cheap laugh. Anybody every tell you slapstick's a dying art?"

"He should know," added Montgomery. "He probably killed it."

Danny clutched the rather dilapidated pile of papers. "Everybody's feeding my complexes today."

Doris and Montgomery took him by the arms, one either side, and walked him away down the corridor.

"Hey, listen," said Doris in a consoling tone, "if you can't let your complexes hang out with your friends, let's face it, who else is going to want you?"

Danny stopped and looked from one friend to the other.

"That helps a lot, fellas, let me tell you."

"Don't knock it," said Doris. "Montgomery here has been spreading your load for you, brother, doing a little part-time

publicising for you all morning."

Danny look disgruntled.

"I kind of wondered who'd been stealing my thunder," he complained.

"But, Danny," said Doris, with a hurt look on her face, "we're only thinking of you. The less organising you have to do, the more time you have to spend on your act."

Danny softened. "Yeah, I suppose so. I hadn't looked at it that way."

"Besides," added Montgomery, with an impish grin, "we reckoned your act might need a little work on it."

Danny sighed in exasperation as Montgomery's and Doris's laughter pealed in his ears. "Friends," he said.

The sound of a guitar wailed and cut across the silence of the room, the notes licking the walls like tongues of flame, snaking back across the floor with an electronic howl as the back beat cut in, punctuating, pointing up the music.

Leroy and Coco moved to the sound of the tape as their movement sliced into the trailing stream of notes, following the punched-

out pattern of the bass and drums. Horns blew, striking out across the landscape of sound, pushing arms and legs in time with the rivetting noise of rock. The music moved into gear…

Coco broke away, stabbed a finger at a button, filled the room with silence, the music vanishing into thin air.

"Can we try that again?" she mused. "I'm not too happy about the way we lead into that last sequence. It doesn't flow right somehow."

"Too jerky," conceded Leroy. "Maybe we need to lead into it earlier, give us more chance to turn and then, wham!—straight in."

"Let's do it," agreed Coco.

She and Leroy had been working over the same phrases of music for the last half hour. Neither appeared to notice the passage of time. They were used to each other's high standards, and neither were happy to leave it, gloss over the problems, until it was just right. Coco rewound the tape.

The guitar split the air once more with its descending wail. The two dancers came alive, shimmered into life, electricity running through their limbs as they connected with the sound.

Unseen, Lydia had entered the room, and stood by the door watching with interest, noting the intense concentration of the faces of her prize students.

Coco stopped the music again.

"How about this?" she asked Leroy, demonstrating her idea. Her eye caught Lydia.

"Don't stop," said Lydia, "it's looking good. Is this for Bruno's?"

"That's right," said Leroy.

"Since you're here," Coco said, "you wouldn't mind watching, would you, maybe giving us a little guidance? It's kind of hard being objective when you're involved in the thing yourself."

Lydia smiled. "Sure honey, go right ahead. I'm watching. Try it once all through so I can get an idea of what you're aiming for."

Coco and Leroy took up positions for the start, having rewound the tape to the beginning. The tape gave a light hiss and ran on through the leader tape until it hit sound. As the music built, and Leroy and Coco went through the steps, Lydia watched with her trained eye, foot tapping to the beat, lyrics running over the melody like a current of water over rocks.

You've got to keep on going
though the way is hard,
those ups and downs
keep going round
right from the start,
and while the end is far away
there is no time to waste I say,
you have to learn your piece
and play the part.

(I'm) doing it now—
You gotta learn how!
Working it out—
There's no room for doubt!
(Just) moving it on—
Come on, let's have fun!
Making it move—
Right along the groove—Yeah!

You've got to keep believing
though it's hard sometimes,
but now and then
the colours blend—
(and) I know it's fine,
and while the heartache's
understood
you know somehow you'll make it
good,
you have to make your star
stand out and shine.

The music ended, dancing ceased, giving way to Lydia's applause. Coco and Leroy looked pleased, knowing Lydia's appreciation would certainly not be insincere, empty praise.

"You two are going to be the star attractions," said Lydia, as she walked over to them. "Just one or two points to make it flow more easily…."

The basement at Bruno's house buzzed with activity. Decorations had transformed the room into a festive grotto, the atmosphere completed with an array of coloured lights which Montgomery had spirited up to illuminate the stage area, and the air was alive

with the noise of electronic humming as Bruno and Montgomery rigged the microphones, amplifiers and speakers that proliferated in the small space.

Danny was running through his routine.

"So the oil sheik sits in the dentist's chair and says, 'Drill anywhere—I feel lucky today', which reminds me of the plastic surgeon who wanted to work in the Middle East, but he could only work at night in case he melted. And then there was—"

"Hey, Danny, Danny!"

It was Doris, looking out of breath, her hair windswept and sprinkled with snow. Danny, annoyed at being interrupted, was about to voice his displeasure, but halted when he saw the worried look on her face.

"It's Coco," said Doris simply. Danny's face dropped: it was bad news. "She slipped on the ice coming out of school tonight and twisted her ankle. I guess her dance number with Leroy is a nonstarter. She's at the doctor's now."

At that moment Lydia was trying to console a very upset Coco who sat nursing her strapped up foot.

"It happens to us all, one time or another," comforted Lydia. "Nobody's fault, honey, it just happens."

"But my number with Leroy at the party tonight," complained Coco. "We worked so hard. Besides which I shall be out of everything for a week or two."

"No use burning yourself up about it," said Leroy, who had been with her when the accident had happened.

"That's right," agreed Lydia. "What's done is done. Sometimes we have to face up to disappointments and just accept them. Something happens and there's no going back, no way, so you have to take what comes and settle for the way it is."

"Could have been your head you fell on," suggested Leroy helpfully.

Coco grinned despite herself. "Thanks, Leroy, glad to know you care." The three of them shared a friendly giggle.

"Nobody's blaming you," Lydia went on. "Anyhow, I don't see that this stops you from going to the party and having a good time."

"The show must go on," smiled Coco, a tinge of bitterness creeping into the edge of her voice.

"That's right, sister," said Lydia firmly, and she winked at Leroy. "I think we might just find a replacement partner for this dancer here… if I can remember all the steps."

The applause died down. The show was over' and the party hummed happily. A group of people surrounded the seated figure of Coco.

"What's the verdict then," asked Doris, "as guest critic of the evening?"

Coco, her spirits revived, looked round her circle of friends. They waited expectantly. "Well," she began, "I do believe Mr. Amatullo actually made me laugh, and as for Miss Grant—I'd say my understudy has a great future as a dancer."

Clapping and laughter mingled together, and outside a fresh fall of snow was drifting downward from a bright sky.

DEBBIE ALLEN PLAYS LYDIA

Debbie Allen plays the beautiful and talented dancer Lydia, *in Fame*.

She was born in Houston, and she is an accomplished actress, singer, dancer and choreographer. Said director Michael Kelljan of her: "Her accomplishments read like the entire cast of a Broadway show."

She graduated with a BA degree in Fine Arts from the Howard University in Washington D.C., and spent her free time from studies working at ballet.

An important step in the careers of many performers in the USA is landing a role on Broadway, and Debbie did that in the chorus line of a hit show, *Purlie.* That led to other roles and choreography assignments, and also the acting part of Alex Haley's first wife in *Roots: The Next Generations.*

Debbie's sister Phylicia, and her brothers Tex and Huey, are also working on careers in showbusiness, and no doubt hoping that they too will soon land such a plum role as Debbie's in *Fame.*

The auditions for *Fame* were stiff—some of the stiffest ever—but watching Debbie's inspired performance in the role of Lydia it's easy to see why they picked this very accomplished young lady for this important part.

LEE CURRERI PLAYS BRUNO

Lee Curreri feels a great bond with Bruno, the character he plays in *Fame*, because in many ways he feels that the two of them, and their lifestyles, are alike.

A native New Yorker, Lee pays tribute to his parents for encouraging and supporting him in his career, even though at times they felt that it was a risky venture in terms of job security.

Says Lee: "In retrospect, at the age of 19, I think that my mother and father felt that music and the performing arts were a hobby... and that I would eventually settle into something more substantial... with a weekly pay cheque."

Hoping to combine his love of music with an acting career, Lee is working with a band he has formed, called Lee Curreri and Modern Times, and he is also interested in songwriting and film scores. Lee also has a great enthusiasm for classical music, and one of his recent successes was helping to arrange and perform the incidental music of Chekhov's *The Seagull*.

Lee has plenty of ideas for the future, but just for the moment he's enjoying bringing the role of the talented Bruno beautifully to life in *Fame*.

ALL IT TAKES

Morning in New York City. Through man-made canyons of steel and glass unknown millions pour along the city streets by car, on foot, by bus or taxi, or underground by subway. New Yorkers, long-time residents, immigrants, visitors, newcomers; all bound on some purpose, the daily swell of activity, like blood coursing through the city's heart.

The lifestyle of a city, pattern of many lives: the executive, career conscious, striding to his office up the ladder of promotion; the gas station attendant, content to sit and watch the world go by; many such lives. But for some, a very few, their choice of direction in life is a leap in the dark along the punishing road to fame. Like the students at the School of The Arts.

"Talent?" Angelo Martelli gripped the wheel of his cab while gesturing with his other hand, which clutched a half empty container of coffee. "You got talent. Believe me, I know, Bruno. And so do you."

In the back of the cab Bruno Martelli, his dark head of hair framing his handsome but thoughtful face, nodded and muttered a subdued agreement.

The cab swung round to the right, Mr. Martelli pulling away into the straight, joining the flow of traffic with all the expertise of a lifetime spent driving the streets of New York. Angelo took a mouthful of coffee, swallowed, and smiled contentedly.

"I tell people," he continued, "I tell them how good you are. Bruno Martelli, my son." He half turned to his son to emphasise his point. "They even tell *me* how good you are. What talent, they say! I'm proud of you, Bruno—"

Bruno looked up at him, almost with a sigh of resignation. "Come on, Pop. Enough of the morale boosting, okay? I'm working on it." He smiled and turned away to watch the passing scenery.

Coco Hernandez, her slim figure and vivacious looks conspicuous even amongst the crowd of youngsters, approached the steps of the school, its ornate arched entrance and painted railings seeming strangely out of place as the pulsating sound of Leroy's cassette deck greeted the arriving students. Coco grinned, her eyes glittering as the music filled her ears. The sound rippled through her limbs as she weaved through the swelling body of students.

"Hey! 1903," a voice said in her ear. Danny Amatullo drew alongside her, mimicking the sway of her legs as she danced along to the music. "Only 1903," he repeated, pointing up at the carved numbers above the arches alongside the words 'School of The Arts', "and I thought I was going to be late, my watch says—"

"Clown!" came back from the departing figure of Coco as she homed in on the cassette.

"That could be construed as a

compliment, if you looked at it in the right way," ventured Doris Schwarz, as she and Montgomery joined Danny on the steps. "That's important in this business," she continued, moving up from the street.

"What do you mean?" asked Montgomery, following her. "Like ignoring criticisms, even sarcastic ones?—Sure, you have to be able to take the knocks with the praise—"

Doris turned, cutting him dead with a look that suggested Montgomery might just have interrupted her flow, upstaged her pearl of wisdom. "I was going to say," she resumed with some authority, emphasised by the fact that she towered over Montgomery below her on the step, "that in this business you always have to look on the bright side, see the good in things—"

"Hey, you're right," interjected Danny, as he caught them up at the top of the steps, "that's a compliment, being called a clown. I'm a comedian. Yeah?"

"—even if it comes in such small doses as Mr. Danny Amatullo here," Doris turned on her heel and disappeared into the building.

"It's not easy being a short person," retorted Danny, as she disappeared inside. He turned to Montgomery and shrugged his shoulders as they followed her in.

The yellow cab drew up before the building and disgorged the laden figure of Bruno, burdened down with books and musical arrangements. Mr. Martelli leaned out of his window, watching his son with fatherly concern.

"Remember what your Aunt Beatrice said."

"Sure, Pop, I'll remember."

"Talent and determination, that's what you have to have to make a name for yourself!" Mr. Martelli said finally, half to himself, half to the vanishing Bruno.

First bell was about to ring and the steps had almost cleared of students. Leroy, hat on head, had taken his music with him, and only a scattering of people now climbed hastily to the entrance.

Mr. Martelli put the cab in gear and the taxi pulled away down the street. "Talent and determination. What else does he need?" he said to the world in general, which continued to pass by unheeding.

One only had to look at Shorofsky to sense the man's depth of experience. Music had been his whole life, and he had not pursued it without a certain amount of personal suffering. Yet the vivid flame of life that burned in his eyes behind the thin rimmed glasses belied the conservative dress and white hair of one his age, and demonstrated more amply than any words that in his life music had emerged triumphant, and continued to spark his energy.

It was through pupils like Bruno that Shorofsky gained much of his satisfaction. If Bruno was rebellious, more temperamental than other students in his class it was because he had an immense, burgeoning talent and that was a difficult thing to handle at such an age.

He gazed down at Bruno, seated at the keyboard, the late afternoon sunlight drifting in through the windows of the music practice room.

"So tell me."

Bruno coiled the headphones in his hands. "I guess I feel pressurised. People keep giving me images of myself I have to live up to."

Shorofsky smiled. "They're not images, Mr. Martelli, they are reflections of you, of your talent. People recognise you for what you are—a talented young man."

Bruno shifted uneasily in his seat, his eyes on the keyboard, avoiding his teacher's gaze. "That's what I mean... all the time people expect me to perform, produce... you know what I mean."

The older man paused for a second, the forefinger of his right hand stroking at the white hairs of his beard below his lip. Bruno looked up at the silence and met the keen eyes of Shorofsky peering intently at him. Bruno shrugged.

"You know," he repeated imploringly, seeking an easy cop-out from explaining. Shorofsky stood quiet and attentive.

"So tell me."

Bruno managed a grin at Shorofsky's repeated words. So tell him. Bruno relaxed a little.

"Like my Aunt Beatrice always wanting me to play when she comes over, or Coco wants a new song for the band, and my Pop telling me how proud he is of me and how all I need is determination." He paused. "You know."

"I begin to, Mr. Martelli," began Shorofsky slowly. He paced towards the sunlight, splitting the shimmering beam with his silhouette as he approached the window. He turned and, leaning against the light, his figure framed against the glass, took in Bruno seated in isolation by his keyboard.

"You lack space, room to expand your talent. Too many 'responsibilities', for want of a better word, in the outside world," said Shorofsky as he moved across the room towards Bruno, his finger tapping against his temple, "when all the time you want to escape to your music inside here."

He stood before Bruno, his eyes betraying both fondness and concern. "Am I right?"

Bruno drew in a breath. "Yeah... that sort of thing."

"What you ask is impossible," Shorofsky said swiftly, simply. Before Bruno could respond he continued. "Why impossible? Because with the gift of talent also comes responsibility. The greater the talent the greater the responsibility. People like to hear you play, they want to share your music because of your talent."

Shorofsky took off his glasses and proceeded to polish the lenses with care and precision, musician's hands still light and nimble.

"Every artist," he went on, rhythmically polishing, "must accept that his greatest gift is communication. If you are able to transport your audience, to lift them subtly from their everyday state of mind and introduce them to a world of your own making, you must not then turn round and starve that same audience of your music."

The glasses were replaced once more in front of those keen, knowing eyes. "An artist has to learn that if his music is good he must be prepared to honour his audience's applause."

The band consented, Coco adding the name of the song to the list. "One more."

Nobody said anything for a while.

Half hearted support for one or other of the songs briefly surfaced, and sank back into the background.

"So what do we do for the last number if we don't want to use either of these two?" asked the drummer, voicing the general concensus that neither song really merited inclusion.

"I could ask Bruno to write something for us, I suppose," considered Coco out loud. The band all found this a great idea, and gave it a unanimous vote.

"Since we do have this chance to put some tracks down in a studio we might as well use the best material we can," argued the drummer. "Maybe Bruno would gig with us too if—"

"I doubt it," said Coco. "It'll be hard enough getting him to write a new song in the time left, as it is. That day's the only one we can use the studio."

"Maybe we can just do the tracks we have," suggested someone.

"No way. I can ask him, at least," responded Coco. She chewed on her lower lip in thought. "How about if we make it the title track? We're already doing a couple of Bruno's numbers. Somehow a title track has a kind of extra appeal, don't you think? How can he resist?"

Angelo Martelli sat on the steps of the cellar, a glass of wine in hand. He was not taking his usual pleasure with the wine, however, the pre-

vious half hour's conversation not having agreed with his digestion.

Bruno sat across from his father, his hands working now and again on a unit from his synthesiser. It was difficult to concentrate, the conversation having unsettled him too, and he disconsolately laid his work to one side.

"I can't understand," Mr. Martelli was saying. "Some days I don't know which way you are going. I wonder sometimes if you know yourself."

Bruno sighed with exasperation. "I've only agreed to do it if I have time. I haven't decided yet."

"But that's the whole point, Bruno," said Mr. Martelli. "This morning you've no time for your

*Imagination
That is where my mind feels free
Imagination
It's a land that's made for me*

Coco's figure danced in his mind, the imaginary sound of the band augmenting his own playing, interwoven vocal harmonies, the air electric as the music made its magic....

Bruno ran a hand through his hair, patted it down against his head. "Isn't that just being straightforwardly commercial, giving your audience only what it wants?"

"Only if you make it so, Mr. Martelli," replied Shorofsky, quick to counter Bruno's point. "If you are good then it will show no matter what style of music you choose to express yourself in. You have great potential, but exploring your talent inside your own head is not enough. You cannot learn in a vacuum. You must learn to take the opportunities in life that are offered to you to test that talent. Any situa-

Aunt Beatrice, and tonight you tell me you're maybe making time for this girl. What's so special about this girl?"

"Nothing, Pop. I told you before," Bruno insisted. "It's a band in school, Coco's the singer. They like my music. They have a recording studio lined up for a day, and one of the band knows a guy who's willing to duplicate a few tapes for them."

"So now you're setting up your own recording company," complained Mr. Martelli. "You let this girl, Coco, wind you round her little finger. What do you get from all this? Tell me that."

"I don't want to talk about it any more tonight, Pop. I'm tired." Bruno made as if to leave.

"Don't want to talk about it," echoed Mr. Martelli. "All this money to send you to this school and you don't want to talk about it. Maybe if you played for your Aunt Beatrice once in a while...." His voice drifted away into silent thought.

Bruno stood at the foot of the stairs. The look on his face tightened and he released his grip on the rail. He let out a long breath. A resigned, drawn out sigh.

"All right, Pop. Next time Aunt Beatrice comes over I'll play her some music. Okay?"

Mr. Martelli reacted warmly. "That's good, Bruno. The family likes to hear you play. I like to hear you play."

"Yeah, I know, Pop. You all like to hear me play." His feet sounded on the bottom steps.

"And Bruno?"

Bruno halted on the stairs.

"Make sure you write a good song for Coco."

The private bubble encircled Bruno, a space within which only the music existed. Seated at the keyboard, music pouring from his fingertips, relaying to his private ears, wired for sound.

*Way out beyond the city haze
Far out beyond these city ways
I live a life that's different there
Music, magic fill the air*

*Imagination
That is where my mind feels free
Imagination
It's a place I long to be*

*Don't pull me back, back down to earth
What is it that you think I'm worth?
I try so hard to share my dream—
(But it's) so hard to leave there once you've been*

tion that you find a challenge is one to learn from."

"But what's the challenge in turning out commercial stuff?" asked Bruno. "It's almost too easy."

"Simply turning out commercial stuff, as you put it, is the easy way out, you're quite right," Shorofsky went on. "But don't hide yourself away from it. Explore. Use your talent to influence tastes if you don't like the music they expect from you. Become involved in changing music. Do not learn to become too narrow-minded too young; learn to appreciate others' tastes in music—"

"Like New Wave?" Bruno cut in with a grin.

Shorofsky grinned back. "There are always exceptions," he admitted. "No music that people like, however, should be condemned simply because it's popular, Strauss was popular but we shouldn't hold it against the poor man. Or should I say rich man?"

"I'm not interested in money," said Bruno abruptly.

"But people are interested in your music," Shorofsky began clearing away some musical arrangements. "Use their interest as a discipline for your talent. That's where the determination comes in. If you are determined enough to expand your abilities as a composer, an instrumentalist, to continually set new limits for yourself, then you will make a piece of music your own, whether it's for Coco, your Aunt Beatrice, or anyone."

Shorofsky clutched the bundle of arrangements to his chest. "It makes you use this," he added finally, tapping his temple once more, as he turned to leave the room. He halted at the door. "Incidentally, you are going home tonight, I presume?"

Bruno nodded. "In a little while. Pop's picking me up later."

"Working late?" asked Shorofsky, indicating the keyboard.

"That's right," replied Bruno. "A song Coco asked me to write for the band."

Shorofsky's farewell barely stifled the chuckle that rose to his throat. Mr. Bruno Martelli was a dark horse and no mistake, and the old man warmed himself with the thought all the way back to the staff room.

The lunchroom. A hundred hands unwrapping lunches, drinking coffee, making small talk, heavy rapping.

Lunchtime scenes, a dozen different stories, and Coco, fronting the band, her dynamic figure exploding into the number as the sound burst across the heads of the assembled diners. "IMAG-INATION! IMAG-INATION!"

The room pulsed, a hundred feet, a hundred hands, moved in one motion, tuning into Coco's compulsive performance, rising with the music, letting it flow through them. A towering wave of sound and movement.

"An' this is what bein' a human bein' is about," laughed Leroy as he launched himself on to the impromptu dance floor to add a new dimension to the moment. "Imagination. Let it go—".

Limbs moving with the music as if somehow they were controlled by wires suspended from the notes as they burst into the air, Leroy translated the sound into human, physical terms, dancing, gyrating, stretching, fluid motion. His body crackled with the sound until it was hard to tell whether the band was creating Leroy's dancing, or Leroy was creating the sound. "Imagination. Let it take you—".

The song rose to its climax, the room filled wall to wall with sound; Coco and Leroy, like twin magnetic forces, drew the audience's eyes, voice and body sending ripples outwards to the hands and feet of those who watched and listened.

Loud cheers, applause, the sound of tables banging. Seated by the wall, Doris, Montgomery and Danny eagerly joined in the general uproar.

"The floor show is getting better at this place," remarked Doris, eating her way patiently, in small mouthfuls, through a piece of lettuce topped with cream cheese. "Wish I could say the same for the Menu." She hastened on, stemming any interruptions. "All right, already—so it's self-imposed. Discipline is good for you, you know?"

"Does that include starving yourself to death?" asked Montgomery, looking in disbelief at her lunch. "Is that discipline or masochism in disguise? What do you say, Danny?"

"Never mind what he says," Doris cut in. "Like the song says, use your imagination. I tried imagining myself one size smaller and I liked it, but nothing happened; I find it easier to imagine this is a three course meal instead, and it's much more effective."

"You worry about being too big," complained Danny. "What about me? What do I imagine?"

"That if you encourage people to diet they'll all get smaller," suggested Montgomery.

"I'd listen to you," volunteered Doris, taking another minute mouthful from her banquet.

Someone had put a tape on and groups were beginning to dance to it in various parts of the room.

Doris, using her lettuce leaf to emphasise her point, said, "You have to look on the bright side, it's the only way." She wagged the lettuce leaf threateningly at Danny. "I believe I can get myself down another size—if I didn't there would be no point to dieting in the first place. Without an optimistic viewpoint you don't get anywhere."

"But you're torturing yourself," laughed Montgomery. "You can tell. You hate every minute of it."

Doris retracted her lettuce leaf, consuming another mouthful. "With friends like you to support me," she began, and bit off the second half of the sentence with a large clot of cream cheese.

"Doris has a point," said Danny. "We're sitting here hoping to make it to the top, but it's so far away you can't see it, so you have to imagine it so you know what it is you're heading for."

One of the band passed their table, a number of cassettes bulging in his pockets. He slid one across the table to them.

"Latest release. Hot from the presses. Featuring the music of Mr. Bruno Martelli, and the renowned Miss Coco Hernandez on vocals. Grab it while it's hot guys. Limited edition.''

Montgomery reached in his pocket, but Doris stolidly ate on through her lettuce. "I'll listen to his copy," she said in between bites. "Imagination I have. Money I don't."

ERICA GIMPEL PLAYS COCO

The old tradition of the showbiz professional being 'born in a trunk' came as near as it possibly could to being true in the case of Erica Gimpel. She comes from a family background of the theatre, and spent much of her early childhood touring with her mother in Australia, Portugal and the States.

Erica was one of the members of the cast who actually was a pupil at The School of The Arts when she was cast in the role of a student there.

She loves drama, dance and music, and in her free time is a keen rollerskater.

P.R. PAUL PLAYS MONTGOMERY

P.R. Paul has a favourite hobby which doesn't exactly endear him to his neighbours: he just loves playing the drums!

P.R.'s acting career is going well at the moment with *Fame*, TV and film roles, and plenty of work in commercials — and he is saving most of the proceeds, towards building a soundproof room for his drumming. "You can't find too many neighbours who're sympathetic to drummers," says P.R.

FALL GUY

a laugh yet?" She gestured to the class out front, who certainly seemed to be more entertained by the argument than they had been by the acting.

Crandall clapped his hands. The bickering stopped. "One thing you both have to learn is that acting is about co-operating with other people. Rehearsal can be a place for argument, but only if it's constructive."

Doris and Danny were suitably subdued.

"All right," continued Crandall. "Let's try it one more time. Doris—try to remember your character's just lost her husband—"

"Yeah, I know," interrupted Doris. "That's what bothers me. What's so funny about that?"

Julie's cousin was a year younger than her, shorter, with

"I don't get the joke," said Doris, halting in mid-sentence and holding the book away from her as if looking at it from a different angle might yield some secret clue.

Crandall got up from his chair and walked over to the group of rehearsing students. He liked teaching drama. It was a satisfying experience to watch young talent grow, to see how his young students explored their capabilities.

He enjoyed using his skill, moulding future actors from such dedicated youngsters. Both Doris and Danny had potential, a natural ability. Right at this moment, however, Doris was looking puzzled.

"Just play it like it's written, Doris," protested Danny. "It's a funny scene, the lines speak for themselves. Just say them, it'll get a laugh."

"That's not good enough," countered Doris. "I'm supposed to understand what I'm saying, don't you see. If I can't see why it's funny then I can't make it funny for an audience, period. I'm supposed to be an actor not a robot."

Danny was about to make a remark he'd regret when Crandall intervened. "Hold it, Doris has a point, Danny. The actor's job is to interpret a script, it's not just a question of accepting the playwright's word that a line is funny and then saying it. An actor has to make the line funny for himself, understand what it says, and then find the best way to demonstrate the joke to the audience."

Danny shrugged disconsolately. "How're we ever going to get this scene together if Doris is too dumb to see what's funny in it?"

Doris uttered what sounded like a snarl. "If you're so good," she gritted, "how come you ain't raised shoulder length hair and glasses. A rather studious but forthright girl, Jackie had always endeavoured to demonstrate some sort of superiority over her older cousin, and Julie's success at winning a place at the School of the Arts did not impress her in the least.

Although Julie's mother had approved of Julie's decision to launch herself along the road to being a threatre professional, some mutterings among the relatives, notably on her father's side, suggested it had not been an altogether wise move. Theatre was not quite the profession into which a member of the Miller family was expected to go; for them it was definitely not respectable. Her father, divorced from her mother, had been silently disapproving.

"But what will you do for a living?" Jackie's mother had asked Julie the last time they had spoken, as if Julie were taking some part time classes in a hobby she planned to take up.

It was an attitude she found all too common among her relatives. The idea of actually earning a living in such a precarious business was wholly incomprehensible to them. When it had first arisen they had gently ignored it as a passing phase, like dolls or horses, but when Julie had persisted she had

been met by blank disbelief that she could possibly be choosing such a career.

It had often puzzled Julie that all the ballet and music lessons had been enthusiastically supported when she was younger, and yet when it came to using that talent to carve out a future for herself several of these same relatives had held up their hands in horror. And to come to a school in New York full of theatricals...! There was much shaking of heads as to her undisputed, subsequent fate.

"Your mother, does she really think it was a good idea your coming to this school?"

Jackie was reclined on Julie's bed reading a book. The bridge of her nose showed small, rosy indentations where her glasses had nestled themselves a home. She pushed the glasses back up her

nose and looked at her cousin. "Huh?"

Julie was seated at her writing table, books scattered across its surface, a pen poised thoughtfully in her hand. "I'm sorry, what did you say?"

"This school you go to—doesn't your mother think it's kind of weird?" asked Jackie, putting her book to one side, her place safely remembered with a book mark.

Julie put her pen down and turned in her chair to face the bed. "Why should she? I do all my regular schoolwork along with the other stuff—I know the capital of Yugoslavia, the date of the Gettysburg Address, how many eggs make a dozen; I just happen to be learning about music and dance and theatre at the same time." She turned back to her work.

Jackie remained unconvinced. "My Mom and Dad would go wild if I told them I wanted to do something as weird as that. Not that I would."

"Not that you would," echoed Julie. "It's what I'm good at, Jackie, it's what I want to do."

"Yeah, well it's still kind of weird," said Jackie, still suspicious. "My Mom says you can read about it in the papers every day of the week."

"Read what?" asked Julie, exasperatedly throwing her pen down.

"Oh, you know," replied Jackie. "Weird stuff. About people in theatre, movies, that kind of stuff. Divorces. All night parties. Gambling."

"Not much of that happening down at the school right now," Julie responded. "We're all kind of busy working. Like I would be if vacationing cousins would put their head in a book and leave me to finish my homework."

Leroy pocketed the coins and put the playing cards back in the pack as the game broke up and the losers dispersed into the steady flow of students. The laid back throbbing of a reggae beat gave the school entrance a welcoming atmosphere, several of the new arrivals stopping to listen and exchange greetings on the steps as the crowd filtered in.

Doris emerged from her locker behind a stack of books as high as her chin. They wobbled a little as she straightened up, but she countered it with some deft juggling and kicked the door of her locker shut with a flick of her foot, drawing an admonishing look from a passing member of staff.

"Hi, Doris."

"Oh, hi, Julie," replied Doris from behind her barricade.

"This is my cousin Jackie," continued Julie without delay. "She's on vacation in New York for the weekend. I thought I'd show her the school while she's here."

"Cultural tour, huh?" grinned Doris. "Listen, I have to love you and leave you, busy day ahead."

"I can see," smiled Julie. "Are you short of a step ladder or is this some light reading to while away your leisure hours?"

"Light reading? Are you kidding? You should feel the weight of these things," said Doris jokingly. "Don't let anyone ever tell you that comedy is a laughing matter. Just give them this bundle to read."

Jackie hung on the edge of the conversation, distracted by the reggae music, looking away at passing people with a critical air, only half aware of what Doris was saying.

"I'm trying to find out exactly what comedy is," explained Doris, with an earnest expression.

"When's this for?" asked Julie, weighing up the amount of reading Doris seemed to be contemplating. "What's today? Friday." Doris reckoned hastily in her head. "Four days, including the weekend."

The warning bell cut across the reggae, and the place seemed suddenly once more like a school.

"Must run," said Doris. "Bye, Julie. Nice talking to you, Jackie. Catch you later."

She rushed off down the corridor, weaving from side to side to avoid people in her haste, tilting and balancing her precarious pile of books as she ran.

Julie laughed. "That was Doris."

Jackie raised an eyebrow. "Uhuh. Hadn't we better go? You'll be late for class."

Coco and one or two of the other girls were gathered round the piano singing vocal harmonies. At the other end of the room a radio played soul music to a small group round the table reading the trade papers. The noise and bustle of lunch hour.

Montgomery deposited his lunch on the table and pulled up a chair alongside Danny, who was in conversation with a good looking girl from another class. She rose and left as Montgomery joined them, but Danny seemed unconcerned.

"Some witch," whistled Montgomery, watching her disappear from view. "Hey, sorry if I butted in on you there—"

"No sweat," said Danny, returning to his sandwich and coffee. "She hates comedians, and doesn't date anybody under five feet eleven. I couldn't disillusion the girl by standing up now, could I? You saved me the trouble. Now she'll always remember me as tall and unattainable. I like that better than small and rejected."

Montgomery began to eat and Danny took a swallow of coffee. In between mouthfuls Montgomery stopped and tried to catch glimpses of the front page of the copy of *'Backstage'* being read by someone on the table opposite, but the newspaper kept jumping about and he couldn't focus long enough to read more than disjointed words, so he gave it up.

Danny continued eating contentedly, watching the diverse events in progress around the lunchroom.

"Are you and Doris back on speaking terms?" asked Montgomery, joining Danny people-watching.

Danny chewed slowly and took his time replying. Brushing the crumbs from his chin, and sitting back in his chair, his face took on a frowning look.

"I'm worried about Doris," he said.

"Worried? What's the matter with her?" replied Montgomery,

drawing his eyes from another 'witch' he'd spotted.

"All this stuff with her acting," Danny went on. "What's she going to learn from all this theory she's filling herself with? Either you have the feel for comedy or you don't."

Montgomery considered this. "That's not fair on Doris," he decided. "She's really into comedy, she just takes it seriously, that's all."

Danny sighed. "Seriously! I'm supposed to play comedy opposite Lady Macbeth? How do I get a laugh when Doris thinks she's playing tragedy?"

Doris added herself to the table, sitting opposite Montgomery, who smiled a welcome.

"We were just talking of you."

"I heard."

Doris levelled a cutting glance at Danny. He stared back defiantly.

"The way I see it," began

Montgomery, thinking to spread oil on troubled waters... but whatever his theory was it never reached the light of day. One look at Danny and Doris told him there was no way he was going to promote a rational conversation between them. The table lapsed into an uncomfortable silence, noticeable even with the background music.

Montgomery cleared his throat nervously, wishing he had something to go and organise so he could excuse himself. To his immense relief he saw Julie standing with Jackie looking for somewhere to sit. From the way that he waved his arms round like a demented windmill it was impossible for Julie to miss him, and the two girls duly took their places at the table.

"This is my cousin Jackie," introduced Julie. "You already know Doris."

"The only actress I know who can whistle *Marching Through Georgia* while eating a hamburger and beating a tambourine with her foot, and still make it sound like Shakespearian tragedy," said Danny unexpectedly.

Doris grew a foot and a half in her seat. Through clenched teeth she replied, "And this is Danny 'the mouth' Amatullo, New York's answer to new wave comedy. Instead of having throwaway gags, you get to keep the gags and throw away the comedian."

"Okay."

"All right."

Both now standing, glaring defiance at each other, they turned on their heels and headed off in opposite directions.

"Hi," said Montgomery, raising a rather weak smile to his lips. "I'm Montgomery, the sane one. How are you enjoying your stay in New York?"

"Weird." The music grew louder.

Down at the Mind Exchange
they're doing something strange;
I can't believe my eyes,
but now I'll put you wise:
it's something you can do
to make a different you;
You just relax your hold
and let them take control—
Change your mind (don't be blind)
Exchange a thought or two,
Then you'll find (right on line)
You've found a thought that's new
Down,
Hey, down at the Mind Exchange
Down at the Mind Exchange
they offer something strange;
they give you new ideas
(but) you leave your old ones here.
Don't let it be supposed
that 'cos your mind is closed
they won't, without delay,
declare an open day—
Change your mind (don't be blind)
Exchange a thought or two,
Then you'll find (right on line)
A thought that's new to you
Down,
Hey, down at the Mind Exchange.

"Well, Jackie, how are you enjoying your stay in New York?"

"It's...er...really interesting," replied Jackie, handing the sugar bowl back to Julie's mother, "but I think I'd find it difficult to live here."

"Oh, why's that, Jackie?" asked Mrs. Miller, relaxing in her chair after the meal.

"Oh, I don't know," said Jackie, pondering the reasons. "I guess it's because everything and everybody seems to move so fast here. You know what I mean?—like life back home is real life, and here it's some kind of crazy, speeded-up version."

"That's one way of looking at it," conceded Julie's mother smiling. "And what did you think of Julie's school?"

Julie made a grimace which was picked up by her mother. "Don't mind your cousin, Jackie," she said. "Go right ahead. It would be interesting to hear what you thought."

Jackie gave Julie a rather smug little smile with her eyes, as if she'd scored a point. "It's like I was saying about the city—it's fast and

crazy. All that loud music, on the steps, in the lunchroom. And some of the weirdest people you ever met. Honestly, I don't know how Julie manages to work in such an atmosphere. I know I couldn't."

Julie rolled her eyeballs to the ceiling, and bit her teeth tightly together. She didn't need to look at her mother to know her reaction. She shot a daggered look at Jackie, and excused herself from the table, disappearing to her room.

"I hope I haven't upset her," said Jackie, affecting a show of concern. "It's true though. There were these two students at our table in the lunchroom…"

It was dark in the apartment save for one table lamp that glowed brightly in the window. Julie sat in the chair, wrapped in

her bath robe and night clothes, reading a book.

The door into the room creaked slightly.

"Julie—is that you?"

Her mother's voice made her look up. Mrs. Miller came into the room, a rather worried frown on her face.

"It's past three o'clock, Julie," said her mother as she saw Julie in the chair. "What on earth are you doing up at this hour?"

Julie smiled apologetically. "I couldn't sleep. I thought if I read for a while I might feel more in the mood. I'm sorry, I didn't mean to disturb anyone."

Her mother took a seat and looked closely at her daughter. Julie felt a little uncomfortable at the scrutiny, knowing her mother's uncanny sixth sense.

"That business at the dinner table isn't still worrying you, is it?" she asked, hitting directly on target. "You don't want to take any notice of your cousin. She has a rather superior way of looking at things. I don't take her views seriously without thinking. I've seen how you've begun to blossom since you came here, and I know

it's not been easy for you. I'm very proud of you, Julie. So is your father."

She laid her hand on Julie's and gave it a small, affectionate squeeze.

"Just think," she said, "when Jackie's forty-two, and just sitting in some office behind a desk wondering why her life is so dull, you'll be playing the concert halls of Europe. Don't let her tarnish your star, darling, she simply doesn't understand. You'll see— you'll have the last laugh."

"Mom," Julie closed her other hand over her mother's, "I love you, but you know what you are?"

"No, what?"

"Weird."

The drama class was assembling itself for the morning's lesson. Copies of the play appeared from bags and their pages rustled as places were found.

Julie looked up to see Doris in a bright and cheerful mood, eager to begin work on the scene again.

"That cousin of yours gone home?" asked Doris, scanning over the pages.

"Jackie. Yeah. And am I glad!" laughed Julie. "She has this one track idea about brains and degrees and diplomas. I mean, sure she's intelligent and that's great, but she just doesn't seem to be able to see that other kinds of talent are just as valid."

"That's the way it goes," said Doris philosophically. "Einstein couldn't tap dance either."

Mr. Crandall made his presence felt and the class fell into silence while he detailed the morning's work. Some slight rearrangement to the furniture and the room was set for rehearsal.

"Has anyone seen Danny Amatullo today?" Crandall asked, noticing his very obvious absence from the assembled actors.

"Yeah, I was with him last period," said a student on the front row. "He was right behind me as we came past the library."

Crandall considered this. "No doubt Mr. Amatullo will deign to make an appearance before long and grace our little play with his performance." The class were suitably amused on cue. "In the meantime we amateurs will struggle on without his expert guidance."

Doris took up her position for her entrance while another student was detailed to stand in for Danny.

"When you're ready."

Doris walked onstage and stopped. She looked at Crandall. "Can I say something first?"

Crandall exhaled despairingly "Go ahead."

Doris bit her lip, took a breath, and began. "You see, I've been doing a lot of reading up and thinking since last week. The way I see it, comedy is always about somebody else's misfortune—we see a guy fall on a banana skin, we laugh; Bob Hope, Bing Crosby, the 'Road' films—we laugh because they're always in trouble. Same with Laurel and Hardy."

Crandall was listening with interest. Doris continued.

"Some really horrible things happen in comedy, or at least they would be in real life. Take Mel Brooks—he even makes us think the Spanish Inquisition or Hitler's a joke. So anyway, this woman I'm playing has just lost her husband. Right? And the joke is she didn't mean to kill him, but Danny's character instead. Right?"

"Right."

"I get the joke," said Doris. "Let's go."

"Ah, Mr. Amatullo," said Crandall, noticing Danny's late arrival as he staggered in with a mountain of books.

"Just been doing a little research, Mr. Crandall," Danny explained hopefully. "Theory of comedy. All that. I've been thinking about what Doris said last week. She's right—it's not funny."

GENE ANTHONY RAY PLAYS LEROY

A 'natural' in every sense of the word, Gene Anthony Ray left cinema audiences breathless when he performed his first stunning dance routine in the film of *Fame,* from which the series was developed.

Now TV audiences too have the chance to see this guy in action — and then some! Gene was such a success in the film that executive producer Gerald Isenberg insisted that he must be re-signed to recreate the character of Leroy in the TV series.

Gene has been a terrific discovery, because not only was he without any formal dance training prior to the film role, but he also created the character he plays largely from his own experiences and intuitive ideas about how the character would behave.

A shy person, and extremely quiet off stage, Gene admits that he 'comes to life' when he's dancing. Even as a youngster he would improvise a dance routine at every possible opportunity, and then retreat to the sidelines afterwards.

Fame has been a fantastic start to Gene Anthony Ray's career, but he is astute enough to know that showbusiness is one career where success is sometimes notoriously brief. "One thing I learned in dancing," he smiles, "is that an encore is as important as your original performance.

"I liked the idea of reprising the Leroy role for television," adds Gene Anthony Ray. "It's like putting on blue jeans and a comfortable pair of shoes… you *know* they fit."

EDGAR ALLAN

Success in a Minor Key

black hole and finding the world was the same and yet not the same, familiar yet totally new.

The cello... dancing... she'd done both those in Grand Rapids. And she was doing them in New York but... the place, this city, the school... it was all so different somehow. She was surrounded by dozens of other people of her own age all doing the same things. But it was a different league.

Girls like Coco Hernandez were so good at what they did. Sometimes it inspired Julie, to be working among such talent; other times... other times she felt a little afraid of all this new life, and she thought of Lester and the familiar streets of what had once been home.

"Julie Miller."

The voice came from nowhere.

"Julie Miller—would you care to tell the class what happens at the end of the story?"

"End of the story?" she heard herself say. A vague feeling of panic rose in her throat.

*I*t's quiet here, like it always is this time of year. People come and people go, but mostly people just stay where they are and let the world drift quietly by. I miss you a lot.

Nothing seems quite the same since you left. I guess being in New York must be equally strange for you. From your letters it sounds as if your work schedule is pretty heavy, but I was glad to hear you felt you were getting on top of it at last. By the way, I hope the concert goes well this week.

Do you still miss me as much, even with all these exciting things in your life—

"Oh Lester," murmured Julie, half under her breath, as she finished reading that morning's letter from Grand Rapids beneath the desk during first period English.

Miss Sherwood was writing on the blackboard, explaining something about Edgar Allan Poe's place in American literature. It faded into the background, slipped from Julie's consciousness, as her mind melted back into the past.

The world around her drifted away and she was again in the familiar streets of home, buildings, places, people she'd known for years, grown up with, become accustomed to. She saw Lester, could imagine him standing by her gate, a fond goodnight, the parting kiss.

And then New York. A million miles away. A million trillion light years from Grand Rapids for all it mattered. Lester might just as well be on another planet; she had stepped from one world to another, like walking through a

Miss Sherwood repeated the question once more, this time with a certain edge. Julie swallowed nervously.

"Which story in particular, Miss… any one in particular… or maybe a special…er, story?" A feeling of being caught red-handed by a thousand witnesses, all of whom turn and point at her and say: "She's the one. That's Julie Miller. She's forgotten her lines." Curtain.

Julie stood by her locker, exchanging the books in her hand for some others she needed for history in the next period. Edgar Allan Poe disappeared towards the back, banished from sight under a notebook, an ill omen for the week.

She took a brush from her bag and began to stroke out her long hair, down across her shoulders. She found it relaxing; ever since she was a small child she'd liked its soft, rhythmic undulations… like stroking a cat her mother used to say… so soothing.

"You all right, honey?"

Coco's voice sounded beside her as she stood daydreaming, eyes gazing into her open locker. Julie stepped back into the present, and rapidly finished brushing out her hair.

"Sure. I'm fine. Just thinking."

Coco opened her locker, taking out a towel and shaking it. "Hey, you don't want to mind Miss Sherwood, honey. She ain't down on you. You know your stuff. Poetry. Shakespeare."

"Oh sure, I know it," replied Julie, finishing her transfer of books. She pushed the locker to, closing the door with a firm click. "It's just that—well, there are so many things happening, so much to decide. I don't think I have room in my life for all of them."

Coco eyed her reflectively, folded the towel. "That's city life, sister. You have to learn to go with the flow, tune into all that energy, light up and take off. You'll get used to it, honey. Don't fight it. Go with it."

"I don't feel lit up," complained Julie. "I feel burnt out." She turned to go.

"Let me give you a piece of friendly advice," said Coco, moving closer, catching Julie's arm. "It doesn't get any easier from here on up, hon'. If you can't stand the heat you better get back out the kitchen. Listen. If you weren't good you wouldn't be here, but you've got to give a hundred and two per cent all the time, or you might as well be wishing dishes hoping to be spotted by some famous director. That's Hollywood—*this* is New York."

Julie listened with head bowed.

"It ain't Grand Rapids either, honey," continued Coco, quieter now, more gently. "Stop fighting against what's happening to you. You're disappearing. Come back down to earth and let us know you're here. Don't blow it, honey, get your head straight. Get it together."

With that Coco walked off, leaving Julie wondering if she'd been advised or chastised. She had no

doubt Coco had meant what she said, but there was something hard about Coco that frightened her.

Coco prided herself on her professionalism, and yet there seemed to Julie something too calculating, too competitive about her manner. Life was a race to Coco, do or die, but Julie was less certain. It kept a certain distance between them, Julie finding herself slightly disorientated by Coco's determination, her driving ambition.

She glowed, the talent radiated out of her. You knew when she stepped into a room she was something special. Charisma… an indefinable appeal that drew you to her, made you notice her.

Julie moved off down the corridor, thoughtful, introspective. Something in Coco *knows* she's good. Julie realised she envied Coco her certainty, but she recognised a feeling in herself, bubbling just below the surface, a rising belief that from somewhere would come the inspiration to lift her above these clouds of depression to somewhere lighter, sunnier, where everything was clear. She could feel it, taste it, but it remained fractionally beyond her grasp.

She thought of Lester, but his image seemed faint, far away. She felt in her pocket for the letter, and Coco's words came back to her, "stop fighting what's happening to you." But how?

Many features
seem to pass before my eyes…
The wheel is spinning
and I really must decide
where I'm going
and just who'll be by my side:
it's hard to feel—
the pressure's on

Try to see my view
It's so different for you
and I really cannot say
why I feel like this today
Mounting pressure,
mounting pressure on the brain,
Social measure
of your power to take the strain

All the memories
go round inside my head…
My world is spinning
and I must be clear instead (of)
where it's going
with its many woven threads:
it's hard to think—
the pressure's on

Try to see my view
It's a different place to you
but I really have to say
what it's like to feel this way
Mounting pressure,
mounting pressure brings me
down,
Work and leisure,
it's no good to be alone
Pressure's on,
on and on…

"You're not feeling so good?"

Shorofsky viewed the girl, tilting his head this way and that as if examining the symptoms. Julie relaxed her grip on the cello slightly, a shy smile drifting across her features.

"Nothing. Oh, it's nothing really."

The teacher opened his hand and gestured towards her instrument. "You play like this for me this morning, and you say it's 'nothing really'." He shook his head.

She brushed her hair back and sighed a little. "Teething problems," she said. "It's taking time for me to settle in. This kind of life, the pace—I don't know, I guess it's different from what I've been used to. It'll be a while before I've adjusted."

Shorofsky nodded.

"A little homesick, perhaps."

"Homesick? No, well, yes. Kind of." Julie's face creased with concentration as she tried to explain herself. "It's like, yes, I do miss the place I grew up in, the people I left behind, but then again—"

"Then again, you find yourself in a place which promises to bring your talents out into the sunlight, and suddenly life is full of exciting new futures you'd never really seriously thought of before. A little

overwhelming, shall we say."

Julie smiled her agreement.

"It's funny," she said, "but whenever I remember back home in Grand Rapids I get to thinking of what I'd miss of New York if I went back, and when I think of living here in New York I find myself checking off all the things I miss about Grand Rapids. Isn't that crazy? I don't seem to be quite connected to one place or the other, caught in between. Kind of transitional period, I guess."

Shorofsky's lips broke into a soft whistle, a phrase from the piece Julie had been unsuccessfully playing. "I've lived long enough to know many such changes," he said, turning to her. "I have changed country. For my music. I have changed continent. For my music."

He looked questioningly at the girl. "Was I right? Should I have taken it upon myself to make such vast changes in my life for the sake of my music?" The teacher fell quiet for a moment. "Yes, of course. For my music, anything. I

trust it. It leads, I follow."

Julie mused to herself, touching the strings of the cello to retune them. "What if," she began, continuing her tuning, "I'm not sure... if I have doubts... no clear direction...?"

"That's precisely why you're here, Miss Miller," replied Shorofsky, addressing himself to the cello arrangement in question. "To find out. Trust in your music will come, you know. Play. Once more."

The sweet sound of strings caressed the silent air, in tones so gentle it seemed as if the very room breathed music. Julie's supple fingers, strong, touching notes, the bow moves swiftly, slowly, sliding, waiting. Streams of notes, a torrent of emotion, the cello plays its song. Mellow, solemn, light, reviving, it moves the listener, reveals new visions, sounds so tender, noise like thunder's distant tremble.

Julie pleased Shorofsky. She played with some skill, a natural flair for the instrument which showed immediately in the way she handled the cello, the way the bow became an extension of her arm, her fingers blending with the strings.

Like an instrument herself, she needed tuning by a master, her raw talent balanced, harmonised, made whole. Shorofsky watched her perform, heard her performance, noted the points of style, technique, that must be perfected. There was no doubt: with tuition she had the makings of a fine musician.

"You see," he said, when at last Julie laid down her bow. "That is so much better. Much more conviction, more confidence. You agree?"

Julie took the compliments graciously.

"It's hard to tell if I'm making progress or not."

Shorofsky chuckled. "You young girls. You move from the mid-west to New York. Overnight. You think your mind adjusts that fast? You pick up a cello to learn. Having a cello doesn't make you a cellist, any more than living in New York makes you an expert on New York. It has to be learnt, studied, practised. Patience, Miss Miller."

Julie shrugged with a touch of resignation. "I know. It'll turn out all right; everybody keeps telling me. I guess I just get anxiety attacks. Do you want to hear it again?"

"Hey, you going to the concert Thursday night?"

Doris took a drink of milk while Montgomery demolished the last of his cup cakes.

"You know that's a terrible thing to eat. It could do awful things to your hormone balance."

"What concert?"

Danny eyed Montgomery with mock disdain. He exchanged glances with Doris. "Is this guy dumb or does he never read the bulletin board?"

"Cup cakes. They affect the eyesight," concluded Doris. "The state his bloodstream must be in.

Ugh." She turned away, unable to contemplate the thought.

"Come on, you guys, what concert?"

A conspiratorial moment of agreement passed between Doris and Danny. Montgomery sat back and twirled his thumbs idly round each other.

"Tell the man."

Montgomery nonchalantly tipped forward in his seat. "Oh, you mean the concert on Thursday?"

"Right."

"With Julie playing solo?"

"Right, man."

"Stage managed by the man they all send for when the going gets rough?"

Danny and Doris took this in. "That couldn't be you, by any chance, Montgomery?" asked Doris drily. "You ever considered moving into a permanent apartment in this place?"

"Hot property, baby," drawled Montgomery, tipping an imaginary hat back off his forehead. "And when you're as hot as me you gotta stay loose. Dig?"

"Cary Grant," ventured Danny. Montgomery raised his eyes to heaven despairingly. "Right?"

"Wrong."

"Maybe you should take up

sword-swallowing instead, Montgomery," suggested Doris helpfully. "I guess impressions aren't in your line. Oh, hi, Julie."

Julie filtered over from the food queue and took her place at the table. "Hi, everyone."

"How's rehearsal coming along for your concert piece?" Doris asked, showing interest. "We were just talking about it."

"Just fine," replied Julie, opening a yoghurt.

"Is it going to be good?" enquired Danny, before Doris kicked him under the table. Montgomery covered Danny's yelp of pain.

"Good? Of course it's going to be good. This is Julie Miller." Danny expressed melodramatic surprise. "You mean—"

"Yes—*the* Julie Miller."

Danny's eyes widened. "Wow! The world famous cellist. Tell me, Miss Miller—" (an imaginary microphone springing into his hand) "—something I've often wondered but was always afraid to ask: how do you manage to fit that huge violin under your chin when you play? No, but seriously, folks...."

But Julie hardly heard their friendly laughter, lost in thought.

I'm changing towns, I'm moving on,
There's many miles to go today,
I didn't wanna leave you
But (you knew) I had to go away
(Yes) the calling's getting stronger
And I can't hold back much longer—
The wheel has turned, the moment past,
I guess it must be time
I travelled on
It's getting late, the lights are low,
I sit and think of you tonight,
I don't know what I promised,
But (you know) I had to catch this flight
(Yes) the winds of change are colder
And it makes me feel much older—
Forgotten dreams, a fading glow,
I guess it must be time
I travelled on
Any yet beyond our troubled stars
There burns a love that we both are

*All things must change and some
must die
But not, my lover, you and I*

*It's time, I guess, I travelled on
New faces, places, near and far,
But while my body might be gone
My heart is always where you are*

The afternoon class came and went. Julie, towel around her shoulders, freshened up with some splashes of cold water. She glimpsed her reflection in the mirror, looked more closely. She looked the same. Or perhaps something in the eyes. Yes, the eyes. The windows of the soul, so they say. A more knowing look possibly, a trace of understanding that was not there before.

She carried the thought home with her, unlocked it in the privacy of her own room, and took out her writing paper to reply to Lester.

Lester, perhaps more than anyone, was a measure of her feelings. In her letters to him she could pour out her thoughts in a way that was not possible with anyone else, although her mother tried hard to sympathise. She knew that. But in Lester she had a confidant with whom she could be herself, no secrets.

Even the act of writing seemed to bring comfort, reassurance. In having to explain herself she found that it helped her put things in perspective, reduce things to reasonable proportions, even discover solutions.

She loved the flow of ink on paper, it soothed her. A refuge from the world, a secret rendez-vous, a place in which to draw on energy, renew. She always glowed a little after finishing one of Lester's letters, felt oddly strengthened, fresher than before.

…I thought of you today, Lester, while I played. I remembered how you watched me play that time at school, last summer towards the end of semester, and you said how well I did in front of all those people. Today I sat and played for my teacher, Mr. Shorofsky, just one man, and I played for him ten times, a hundred times

harder than I did back in school that day.

The more I learn, however, the more I realise I don't know yet. Mom keeps saying I have to learn patience and perseverance, and I guess she's right. (I just wish there was a way to learn them instantly!)

Tomorrow night I play in a concert, nothing big, just a small audience, no great occasion. I look at the future and think, when is it going to begin? It seems a long way off. But I sit down and play the cello and—this is going to sound dumb—it feels like I'm a part of it, like I'm the music. Am I weird or does this make sense?

And when I feel that, I know things are going to work out. It can't fail. I can't explain. It just makes me feel so good.

The note seemed to drift on forever. It hung, quivering on the edge of sound, then fell into silence. The mounting ripple of appreciative applause built and broadened, as Julie took her bow,

a glitter of pleasure radiating from her as she acknowledged the warm response.

Shorofsky was waiting for her as she came off stage. "Played like a professional! Room for improvement, many things to learn, but tonight I admired the spirit in which you played." He drew her further into the wings.

"The other day you were not yourself, and it showed in your playing. Tonight... tonight I could not tell. I watched your face and all I saw was a musician transported by her music."

"Thank you," said Julie, her heart still racing with adrenalin from her performance.

"That's not an unqualified compliment," Shorofsky hastened to add. "Now we have a musician who knows that when she works with her music she allows nothing else to divert her concentration. Next we make you a musician who uses that ability as a platform from which to master the instrument. We progress. Miss Miller, we

progress."

"Miss Miller wishes to make no statements to the press as of this time," explained Montgomery to a startled hamburger salesman, as the four of them walked back from the concert.

Julie linked her arms more snugly into those of Doris and Danny. She giggled. She felt on top of the world and she wasn't sure why. A small audience, nothing big. But people had applauded because she played the cello. Maybe it was the renewed sense of identity it gave her, and her friends—such good friends—made her feel gay and light-headed with their make-believe.

"Miss Miller," Danny gasped, racing alongside her, clutching his imaginary microphone. "Do you have a word of advice for all young musicians watching tonight?"

Julie turned and faced the 'camera'.

"Wakka-wakka-wakka."

"More than generous, Miss Miller. Good night, America."

VALERIE LANDSBURG PLAYS DORIS

Valerie Landsburg is the child of showbiz parents, who grew up in the showbiz community of Hollywood, attending Beverley Hills High School, and studying drama.

All the more surprising then, that when she entered college it was to study psychology! Valerie was fascinated by this subject, and she intended to make it her career, until an offer of a part in a film changed her mind. She put her psychology books into storage, and she's been working in showbiz ever since.

Valerie enjoys a challenge, and she has taken on all sorts of different parts with great enthusiasm, including a leading role in a successful Neil Simon comedy, after spending a year understudying the role.

The production side of the business also interests her, and she works at this during her breaks from acting. She has been a production assistant on two films, and she also did the audio research for another production.

Just for now though, it's Doris to whom she is devoting all her energies, and *Fame* is the showcase for her talents.

LOOKING FOR THE MAN

The pool room was hazy with smoke, a long flat cloud hanging above the tables almost as if it were suspensed from the ceiling. The soft babble of voices peppered the fringes of the room, while at the tables men in pairs circled the green baize intent on sending successions of brightly coloured balls into the busy pockets.

Bright light illuminated their endeavours, spilling over onto the surrounding floor, edging its way towards the half-darkened walls. Leroy, taking time out from his chores, sat on a bench, its dark, decrepit woodwork harmonising in a decaying sort of way with the dismal, ageing walls.

He paid no heed to his surroundings, grown distant with familiarity. It was his job and it paid the rent. He asked no questions, cleaned the place up each night as the customers came and went, and left his mind to other things. He didn't like it, paying his way through school like this, but there was no choice and at least it enabled him to do what he most desperately wanted to do: dance.

He knew the route he'd chosen in life was an unusual one, but it was a way out, a way up, a real future. Others like him had taken different ways—like his brother Willard they had taken a downward road through crime, a passing rise in fortune perhaps, but ultimately downward. Leroy knew that, had fought hard against it. Often it had seemed an almost inevitable path, but he had fought it off, struggled through against the odds.

He had won a coveted place at The School of The Arts. His dancing had taken him there, and his dancing would take him further. Sheer determination and a talent driven by the fear of failure and what it would mean to him had made him the dancer he was—vibrant with energy, fired with the will to succeed, eager to learn, improve, move on and up. It fuelled his life; there was only dancing.

He looked rather dismally at the text book in his hands, homework relegated to his free moments, stolen from the nightly business of stemming the tide of refuse that flowed like a continuous tide across the floor of the pool room. The words stayed steadfastly on the page, refusing to come into his mind.

Words, so many words. He understood what music said to him, he felt it rather than thought it. He knew how to express himself, using his body as a writer used his mind. But all these words, so many pages, paragraph following paragraph, sentence upon sentence; he faced a mountain whose heights he could not even guess, let alone scale. He could fly but he could not climb.

That side of school he endured.

It burdened him, made his mind feel heavy, and he longed for the future, that future in which dance would be the whole of his life and books would be a long forgotten nightmare from the past.

The door on the far side of the room swung open, and a tall man, smartly dressed, his suit well cut, made his entrance. Voices nearby dropped low or ceased, the man's presence radiating fear or respect, or both, across the room in ripples until all fell momentarily silent, still, before a quiet nod of his head signalled that he was satisfied by their reverential welcome. The games resumed, the conversations wound up again, though softer now, in whispers, and the man surveyed the place.

Leroy looked up from his book, easily distracted. The man was staring directly at him. Leroy's glance went down immediately to the page before him but he knew

even before he read the next words who the man had come to see.

The tall negro crossed the floor in a measured pace towards the seated boy. He halted before him, invading his space. "Man says your name's Leroy Johnson. That right, boy?"

Loud music punctuated the morning chatter of arriving students. The electronic beat pulsed with a solid, driving force, the sound of a synthesiser building and booming over the backing, its note wheeling, diving, climbing out across its foundations like a soaring arc. Those close to moved to its magic, continuing conversations with each other, while their bodies talked to the music.

Montgomery entered the circle of sound within which all was movement, bodies wired to the machine like puppets on their strings, involuntarily dancing as if its hypnotic spell could not be

broken. Coco stood close to the centre, the sound trembling fluidly through her limbs. Montgomery half danced his way to her, caught by the atmosphere.

"Hi, have you seen Leroy?" he asked, his voice barely piercing the barrier of sound. "He was supposed to turn up early this morning to go through that routine. He hasn't shown up. Do you know where he is?"

Coco shrugged her shoulders without interrupting the flow of her dancing. "No idea," she told him. "Maybe he's sick."

Unenlightened, Montgomery moved off. There were times when he wished he didn't always volunteer to mobilise the forces when some organisation was needed. So much chasing about whenever his charges failed to keep up with his schedules, so much time wasted for everyone when people failed to turn up for rehearsal, leaving others stranded like a football team without a ball. It was frustrating for all concerned, and it made him wonder why he bothered. In this business you had to be able to rely on people.

Still, it was mighty strange about Leroy. As far as anything to do with dancing was concerned Leroy was a man who could be depended on to do all that was required of him and then some. If more rehearsal was required Leroy was top of the list of volunteers. He left others standing when it came to enthusiasm, even though Leroy balanced an obsession for working up to his best with a barely restrained impatience for the performance itself.

Rehearsals with Leroy were driven with a fierce, relentless energy which ultimately exploded on stage.

He must be sick. Montgomery could find no other plausible explanation.

Elizabeth Sherwood sat at her desk in the empty classroom. Another day had passed. Shakespeare, English grammar, the modern novel, a lively debate on nuclear disarmament, rounded off with a lesson on contemporary poetry. A good day, some useful work.

She gathered her papers together, shuffling them into a neat block, and sliding it into the narrow remaining space in her bag between a set of unmarked assignments and a couple of text books.

She glanced at the top page as it disappeared from view. For once Leroy Johnson had turned out a half decent piece of work. She found, with a mild touch of surprise, that she had actually been looking forward to handing it back to him, lavishing a little praise on the boy, something all too rare in her experience of him. She sniffed disappointedly and slid it out of view.

Lydia Grant's head appeared round the edge of the door frame.

"School's out, hon', time that all good teachers hit the road and made for home."

She moved gracefully into the classroom, her own bag bobbing by her side as she walked.

"Hi, Lydia," greeted the English teacher. "Just gathering together the day's harvest of literary masterpieces. I'm all set."

She rose from her chair, slung the bag across her shoulder and joined her colleague, strolling beside her as they went out into the corridor, heading towards the staff room.

"Did you have Leroy today in class?"

"No, I didn't," replied Lydia, half turning her head. "Nobody seemed to know where he was. Why? Don't tell me his head's on the block again."

Miss Sherwood was pleased she was able to surprise Lydia for once. "Quite the reverse, as a matter of fact. He actually turned out quite a remarkable piece of writing for me, a short story. When I say short, of course, I do mean short—"

The two teachers shared a not unkind laugh.

"—but for once it was quite lively, imaginative even, and while his grammar and punctuation don't exactly hit the high spots, it actually reads as if he enjoyed writing it."

Lydia nodded appreciatively. "You think you may be making an impression at last?"

"Hard to say," Miss Sherwood replied as they reached the junction in the corridor and turned off. "I asked the class to write something from their own experience, something that reflected life in New York as they saw it."

"And what was Leroy's contribution?"

Miss Sherwood hesitated momentarily. "Well, I wouldn't say that it's precisely what I asked for, but—"

"So what did Leroy dig up from his murky past to fit the bill?" asked Lydia, intrigued by her companion's reticence.

"I've no idea where he got it from," explained Miss Sherwood as they reached the staff room. "It was about some underworld figure and his rather unsavoury habits."

Lydia couldn't help but laugh out loud. "With Leroy Johnson I wouldn't be surprised if it was lfited word for word out of real life. He doesn't exactly live in the most respectable suburb of town."

They deposited their respective bags on the counter and began putting their coats on. Miss Sherwood took this opinion in, looked doubtful.

"Wherever it sprung from, it's one of the best things he's done for me," she said. A sigh of exasperation escaped from her lips. "You wouldn't believe it, would you—the one time I want to give him a few words of praise and he's not here."

If you want to know the score
there's a man you have to meet—
he's called a thousand names,
he's the voices on the street.
If you need to know the number
then there's just one place to go—
down a hundred different alleys
where the policemen never show.

He's the man, I mean
THE man—
If you want it
Then he's got it
If you fit into his plan.

If there's news, you need to have it
then there's someone sure to tell,
it's the man who makes his living
from the secrets that he sells.
If you cross him, say your prayers,
man,
'cos that's all that's left to do,
you better take the next flight,
he'll be looking out for you.

He's the man, I mean THE man—
If you've got it
And he wants it
Then you better have a plan…
'cos he's the man,
the one and only MAN,
He's the MAN…he's the MAN.

"Three days and no word. Nothing!" complained Montgomery, pacing up and down impatiently. "None of the staff know where he is, and Danny came with me last night to see if he was at his pad—"

"You went down there?" Julie asked, a tremor of disbelief needling up her spine.

"We need to find the guy, don't we?" asked Montgomery insistently. "I can't say it was my idea of a Sunday stroll, but we're short of our best male dancer, and without him we have to scrap the whole number or start again. Okay?"

The tension in his voice plainly showed, and it was obvious that the trip to Leroy's neighbourhood had not been undertaken lightly. Julie backed off gently.

"I was just asking."

"Well, nobody was talking over-much," Montgomery went on, winding himself down a little, "and we didn't want to stick around too long, if you know what I mean, but as far as we could see there was no sign of him, hasn't been seen for a couple of days now. We even checked out the pool hall he works at—seems like everyone's looking for him right now, but nobody's talking."

"So what do we do?" asked Julie. "Has anybody checked the hospitals? Maybe he's been hurt, knocked down or something."

"I asked at the office. They're worried too, and they tried that today when I said he seemed to have disappeared. No joy." Concern was clearly etched on everybody's faces. "They're going to give it one more day, then they'll call the cops in."

All thought of rehearsal disappeared, each wrapped in his or her own imaginings. The group broke up and went their own ways, nobody keen to voice their personal fears.

Elizabeth Sherwood's apartment had a comfortable, lived-in feel about it. Though the place was clean, tidy was not a word you could apply to it. Books lay stacked in sundry piles, some on their way from the shelves, others on their way back, several just passing

44

through. A copy of the previous Sunday's *Times* lay half read on the arm of the couch, and a week's diet of albums clustered round the stereo looking for sleeves to call their own.

A pot of hot coffee stood on the table beside her reclining figure, a half empty cup in one of her hands, a half read book in the other. Some music from the distant sixties drifted tunefully from the stereo, and the atmosphere was relaxed. After work, shoes off, a lazy evening read to end the day.

The knock at the door startled her slightly, bringing her back from the California of the 1930s where her mind had been dreamily wandering amid the pages of the book.

She got up from the couch, placing her open book on a pile at the end of the coffee table, and the coffee cup next to it. She crossed to the door, puzzling as to who could be calling at this late hour.

The door edged open, the safety chain allowing a slit to appear. Leroy stood in the corridor.

"Leroy?"

Leroy looked anxiously left and right. "Can I come in?"

Miss Sherwood instantly picked up his uneasiness and slid off the chain, allowing Leroy to enter, which he did swiftly. The teacher took the situation in her stride, remaining friendly and relaxed, giving him time to slow down, offering him coffee, clearing a seat for him. Leroy had come to talk; there was no need to hurry him.

"I had to come here, Miss Sherwood," he began, after he had drunk his way to the bottom of the cup in quick, large gulps. She refilled it. "I had to let you know why it is I ain't been to school this week."

She allowed the pause to continue, watching Leroy as he wrestled with his words, searching for the right way to say what he had to.

"You know I don't do nothing that ain't legal, Miss Sherwood," he continued earnestly, after some thought. "Going to the school means to much to me; I don't want no trouble."

She nodded her assent, inviting him to continue uninterrupted.

"Sometimes though, no matter what you do, trouble comes looking for you," Leroy went on. "Last week it found me. This dude came into the pool hall. I've seen him around a few times, I know where he's coming from and I beat a wide path around him. Whatever it is he's into, I know it ain't delivering Gideon Bibles."

Miss Sherwood sat forward in her seat, apprehensive about what might be going to follow.

"This night there ain't nothing I can do. He comes right up to me and asks me if I've seen Willard. My...er...brother, you know? I don't have nothing to do with him, you know that, not since the last time he turned up toting that gun. So I told him, but he don't want to take no for an answer. He says Willard's got something of his, a package, I don't know, and he wants it back—he can't find Willard but me he does find."

Leroy took another long gulp of coffee.

"I'm telling you, this dude means business. Threatens to break both my legs if I don't deliver. Says he'll be back in a day or two."

Miss Sherwood held in the shock, biting her lip.

"Go on," she prompted.

"There ain't nothing more I can tell him, and my legs are

something I can't afford to have messed about, so I lit out." Such a threat was all too clearly just about the worse thing Leroy could conceive of happening, given that dancing meant everything to him. "I didn't know what to do. I've been sleeping out in Central Park—I daren't go back to my place, or the pool room, and I figured he might come looking for me at the school...."

"Why didn't you call us?" asked the teacher, her desire to help evident in her tone. "You're not alone, Leroy, you have friends."

"I was confused, I guess," replied Leroy. "Then I finally figured you'd know what to do,

Miss Sherwood, on account of how you helped me over that business with Willard last time."

"You've come to the right store, Leroy," she answered without hesitation. Despite his shortcomings, she had a real affection for Leroy. She admired his spirit, and she knew the constant battle he fought to keep on with what he most believed in. "This is one time the police are going to be right behind you. I'll call them. Can you give a description?"

"You already got one, Miss Sherwood. He's the one I wrote about. You got anything to eat, Miss Sherwood? I'm awful hungry."

"Glad to hear you're off the Mafia hit list," joked Montgomery as he joined Leroy in rehearsal.

Leroy afforded himself a smile. "Me too. Turns out the cops already picked him up for something, couple of nights back."

Julie joined them, giving Leroy a welcoming hug.

"We were so worried about you, Leroy."

"Girl, you weren't the only one," sighed Leroy. "Willard knows some mean dudes, honey, and that's no lie."

Julie looked up at Leroy, slightly in awe. Surely this sort of thing only happened on television, not real life. It seemed strange to feel so close, even at one remove, to what for some people was actually reality.

"Is it true you've been sleeping out in Central Park?" she asked, finding it hard to make all this tangible to her mind.

"All the best people do, girl," grinned Leroy. "A person just ain't educated till he's tried it. It's kind of short on the home comforts, but there's plenty of space to rehearse in."

"Rehearse?"

Both Julie and Montgomery looked at him in amazement.

"That's right," replied Leroy, unruffled. "I think I've just about got this thing worked out. I knew you'd be putting in the rehearsals here, so I figured I better have myself ready, with time being short and all. Shall we try it?"

Julie looked at Montgomery, as if she found it hard to believe Leroy was for real; but he was speechless too.

"Time's awasting, brother and sister," Leroy went on, beginning his warm-up routine. He looked at their startled faces. "There ain't *nothin'* stops me dancin'—don't you know that yet?"

LORI SINGER PLAYS JULIE

Born into a world of music, Lori Singer is the daughter of the famous conductor Jacques Singer, and Lori herself is an accomplished performer. She played as a cello soloist with the Oregon Symphony at the age of 12, and has gained recognition and acclaim for her musical talents.

Not only that, but before *Fame* Lori had an exciting modelling career, with assignments for prestige magazines, including *Vogue*.

But it is in acting that Lori really wants to make her mark, and the role of Julie in *Fame* is an important stepping stone for her. This show looks likely to launch some great stars of the future!

TEAM EFFORT

The polished curve of the face, was in essence feline. All attention was drawn to the eyes, bright emerald green, and the way their sparkling luminescence burst forth, arrowing out beneath the sloping forehead.

Sound, deep thunderous sound, low murmuring notes rolling from a distance, fathoms deep from some subterranean cave. The animal moved.

"And so for this project we will be combining resources, as it were," Elizabeth Sherwood was saying, standing in front of the class with an open loose leaf file in her hands. "In these classes we will be discussing and developing ideas to use, and going on to produce a basic outline. Once we have that, the other aspects of the production can start work on their particular section—at least the dance and music can begin exploring the possibilities we've put forward, while we work in conjunction with the drama class to produce the improvised and scripted dialogue scenes."

The camera closed in on Doris to view her reactions to the English teacher's speech, capturing the obvious interest the girl showed. The director looked pleased. The whole class was behaving as if the video unit wasn't there at all; it gave it the 'fly-on-the-wall' feeling that he was looking for, so that the viewer would become an invisible participant, in the room but watching unobserved.

The tape turned slowly, images collected, stored and taken from the present, winding on to the spool, as the hungry camera devoured still more.

The dance class was scattered round the room, each student in a space, all eyes turned to Lydia as she weaved among them, talking.

"We will then spend two or three days working out our sequences, initially trying to evolve appropriate styles of movement, a basic vocabulary from which we can build once we have the rehearsal tape of the music."

The camera followed her as she moved through the class, her practice skirt swaying as she walked. The sound man made some slight adjustment to his controls, watching the needles as they flickered on the dials.

A thousand small cries splintered the air, nerves vibrated by the unmistakable, shrill utterance of fear. A myriad of small faces scattered like the shimmering of moonlight on a pool, racing out from their neatly ordered group to a far-flung, broken patchwork.

The beast hung motionless, head quivering, ears seemingly tilted into the sound. Its thunderous rumble flowed like dark water beneath the tiny, shrieking notes of its victims.

"This is a group effort," emphasised Shorofsky, peering at his students through his spectacles, "but make no mistake—there is no such thing as democratic music making. We will pool ideas, we will all contribute instrumentally, but the phase in between has to be limited or we will chase each other in circles until we are exhausted. Trying to compose is like making the famous broth—too many cooks will spoil it."

He half smiled at his remark, the camera catching it as he turned his head to address his next remark, the camera catching it as he turned his head to address his next remarks to another section of the class. The director smiled in his turn, knowing he had Shorofsky's unconsciously expressed pleasure on tape. It would be a nice moment to use in the final cut.

The semi-circle of students were grouped around Crandall, the drama teacher, as he sat on the stool explaining their involvement in the project. The cameraman was shooting over his shoulder towards the upturned faces, slowly moving round to take in Crandall's profile.

"We're only talking about ten minutes of actual performance," he said, using his hands to punctuate what he was saying. A finger stabbed out, "So—the emphasis is on being economical and concise. The scenes we shall be doing, including voice-overs, will total somewhere around four to five minutes, in which time we have to put over what we want to say clearly and graphically."

The camera slowly zoomed in, the lens narrowing in from the full length shot of the seated teacher to take in only the head and shoulders.

"We'll begin with improvisation, based on the guidelines laid down by our scriptwriting team in the English department, and once we've evolved some workable dialogue we'll hand it back to them to hone down to a final, polished script. Any questions?"

Slowly, almost imperceptibly, one small figure became separated from the rest. Like the parting of a great sea the others drew aside like two walls of water, leaving a dark tunnel connecting the powerful creature with its puny adversary.

The wail of voices climbed to a crescendo, hanging tremulously in the air, hovering as if it must fall. The ominous, malicious purr ran murderously below it. At their peak the shrill voices of fear vanished into the rolling tones of the beast, a solitary crying sound pinned starkly against the thunder. The animal slowly closed in for the kill.

Lydia poured the coffee from the pot and everybody bent forward to take their cup. Miss Sherwood sat next to Lydia, Shorofsky and Crandall reclining on the couch across the room, and the director and the members of his crew interspaced between the two pairs of teachers on chairs and cushions. The conference was lively, an air of excitement evident in the room.

"The students are really into the project," Crandall explained, spooning sugar into his coffee.

"Absolutely," agreed Sherwood. "They really seem taken with the challenge of trying to make a statement, tell a story within the ten minutes time limit."

"Like we were saying earlier," Lydia continued, finishing pouring and putting down the pot, "their awareness of the disciplines involved in producing a short video has come on remarkably quickly."

"They're responding very professionally," agreed the director. "I've been very impressed by how fast they've grasped the basic limitations of video as well as its possibilities. I think they will produce a very watchable piece of work."

The company all voiced their agreement.

"What we have so far then," Elizabeth Sherwood said over the murmur of voices, "is the central theme of the scapegoat. The idea is to use the image of the one animal sacrificed to the hunting cat so that the others can avoid the same fate—"

"We're using that as the basis for our dance and movement sequences," interjected Lydia.

"—and to take the same idea, but translated into human terms, in the acted scenes," Miss Sherwood continued, "intercutting the animal and human sequences so that they develop along parallel lines."

"We have the basic story line worked out now," Crandall put in, "and at least two out of the three

scenes, I'd say, are close to the point where we could turn them over for final scripting." The director nodded.

"That leaves us with the closing sequence," Miss Sherwood concluded, "in which we combine animals and humans in such a way that brings the two elements of the video together and moves to the climax."

"How about the voice-overs?" asked the sound technician.

Crandall answered. "The latest on that is that the students want to have a taped voice over the opening sequence of grazing animals, and also one over the first shot we have of the humans, simply to introduce the basic ideas and link the two elements together. They think they'll probably want some sort of speech played over the last image that we hold on, to point the statement they're making."

"No sweat," replied the sound man.

"What stage is the music at, would

you say?" asked the director, turning to Shorofsky who had been quietly drinking his coffee, taking in the discussion.

"Quite advanced," he answered, replacing the cup in its saucer. "Miss Grant now has the basic soundtrack we've recorded and is working to that. At the moment we're experimenting with various instruments to see how we can embellish the sound, make it more expressive. I must say they're producing some quite startling noises!"

His rather pained expression prompted laughter from several of the others. "You know what they say about suffering for your art," quipped Lydia, and the meeting rebounded with further good-hearted chuckles.

"Now, about next week," said the director, when the amusement had died down. "I've worked out a provisional shooting schedule you might like to look at...."

World of instant images
taken where you will,
laid upon a moving tape,
developing the skill—
view it, shoot it, tape it,
play it back to see,
technology's provided
your own film company
It's a video revolution
Everyone can have their fill
You make your contribution
Everyone becomes de Mille!
A world within the grasp of all,
VTR is here,
don't need to be in Hollywood
to make your own career,
(you can) buy it, rent it, use it
won't take a millionaire,
video's for everyone,
a miracle to share
It's a video revolution
leaves all rivals standing still
Fulfil your own illusions
Be like Cecil B. de Mille!

"It's a great idea," said Danny enthusiastically. "I wonder who asked the Video Workshop to come here in the first place?"

"I hear it was they who approached the school," replied Julie, as they sat with Doris and Montgomery on the school steps, watching the world go by. "Some guy there thought it would make a neat documentary to film us putting a video together."

"Miss Sherwood says they plan to show it round schools," chimed in Doris, "to give kids an opportunity to see what kind of things you can do with video, how it's put together. I can't wait to see the finished thing."

"Star struck," grinned Montgomery.

" 'Fame hasn't changed my life at all,' says video star Doris Schwarz," added Danny, reading an imaginary newspaper headline.

"Come on, you guys," protested Doris. "You're every bit as excited as I am, you can't fool me. It may not be the real thing, not prime time television, or a multi-million dollar blockbuster, but we're still making a video and you'll be fighting for the front row seats to see yourself just the same as the rest of us."

The others nodded agreement unhesitatingly.

"And what's more it's going to be good," said Danny with conviction in his voice.

"Yeah," Montgomery said. "That idea of yours for the video was something else, Julie. Where did it come from?"

Julie blushed slightly, although the compliment gave her a great deal of pleasure. Modestly she replied, "I suppose it was the school itself, the way everybody gets along so well, no matter what the colour or the race of the individual. It's like everyone knows there's more important things in life—so we don't single out people because they're not the same as us and make them take the blame when things go wrong."

"Julie's right," said Doris, joining in. "We work together. The kind of thing we do, we will be doing— shows, films, whatever—relies on everybody helping each other. If one element of a show isn't working the whole show doesn't work—it's no good throwing all the blame on the person, you just have to work together to bring out the best in everyone so you can overcome the problem, whatever it might be."

Montgomery looked thoughtful. "Isn't it that our line of business is a particularly unusual blend of the individual and the group?"

"How's that?" asked Doris.

"I mean we need to encourage individuality—that's what makes a great dancer or a great actor or musician—but at the same time as being allowed to develop our own individual talent we also have to learn how to use it in conjunction with others, in a dance troupe or an acting company."

"There's more to it than that," said Danny, coming into the conversation. "Surely it's the fact that we all have the same goal, the best combination of all our talents, in a production. We're taught to approach problems constructively, because a solution's in all our interests, instead of shifting the blame to the weakest link. If a show's a flop everyone's responsible, so everyone has to work to make it come good. Isn't that the point of it, Julie?"

Julie raised her eyebrows and pondered for a moment. She laugh-

ed. "I can't say all that passed through my head at the time, but I guess it all applies. The idea of the animal which the rest of the herd sacrifices, and the guy that gets the same treatment in the other scenes, is just how I thought the world seems to operate. Instead of all working together to solve the problems everyone sits round looking for someone to blame for why it's gone wrong or why they can't do anything about it. It seems to me we operate differently here; if we tackled doing plays or dance routines like politicians run the world, theatre would be dead in a week—we'd never get anything together."

"Talking about getting things together," said Danny, looking at his watch, "we have a class in twenty-five minutes and Miss Sherwood's going to want to know how we're going to end this thing. We still haven't settled the final scene. Where's that script?"

Bruno sat and listened to the music, unmistakably pleased by what he heard, yet even more impressed by what he saw. Given his gift for composing, he had been the driving force behind putting together the music for the video, and yet while he had at first baulked at the idea of not working alone he had found to his surprise that the exchange of ideas with the others had actuallly inspired him, given him fresh thoughts, created new avenues to explore.

He had not had a lot of experience writing music for theatre as such, most of his compositions to date being designed with a musician or singer in mind. Now, as he watched the dancers interpreting the imaginative soundtrack—part atmospherics, part straight music— and allowed his mind to wander back over the cross-fertilisation of ideas that working with dancers and actors had produced, he acknowledged what a rich experience he had found it.

People had danced to his music before, of course, but only in response to a completed piece of work, something that had been perfected even before they had heard it. In this case, the development of the music and dance, of the drama and the sound backing, had

been a two-way process from the start, each medium feeding the other as the ideas progressed. He could tell Shorofsky was pleased, and this in turn pleased him. He knew he'd done a good job, made a positive contribution, and he felt he'd gained a lot from it.

To watch the dancers add their own dimension to what he'd helped create gave him a special pleasure he could not remember experiencing in quite the same way before. The cameras rolled as he watched, and Lydia too looked on appreciatively at what the students had combined to produce. She shared a smile of pleasure with Elizabeth Sherwood. Crandall caught their eyes at the same moment, and it was evident that he was inpressed with the end result as well.

Students writing, choreographing, composing, students acting, dancing, playing, even students operating cameras, and the lights and sound. They had produced, if not the greatest ten minutes of do-it-yourself video, at least something which promised potentially accomplished work in the future. In a world of entertainment fast coming under the domination of the omnipresent electronic eye, it was a skill all these budding entertainers would need to have.

Shorofsky sat quietly observing as the student company did a last take on the closing scene. The level of work, he considered, was high, in all departments, but he had been particularly impressed by what the students had chosen to put their talents to work for.

The familiar closing moments were played out before him. Two circles of masked figures, one human, one animal, moved round in opposite directions, a protective double ring around the enclosed solitary figures of the twin scapegoats. Outside the circles the beasts, in both human and animal form, tried in vain to break through and devour their victims, but were repulsed.

The words of the final statement, to be taped and added in later, ran fluently through his mind. "United we stand, divided we fall. If we always allow the mass to prosper at the expense of the individual, we will all perish one by one. To choose a scapegoat is not to defeat our foe; it merely delays our own destruction. Only together may we survive."

The music rose in triumphal victory and he found himself strangely moved. An ancient ideal, a simple statement, but he was glad to see his students were learning not only to be artists but people too.

The video ends and fades to black.

CAROL MAYO JENKINS PLAYS MISS SHERWOOD

Carol Mayo Jenkins was an experienced and successful actress in shows from Broadway to San Francisco before she was cast for the part of Miss Sherwood in *Fame.*

She loves the part, and finds it creatively rewarding, but there is still one thing she misses about playing to cameras rather than a live audience, and that is the sound of applause.

Says Carol: "More than ever in my career, people recognise me in the street, but that's just not the same as actually feeling audience reactions and taking a bow to the sound of applause."

Even so, Carol feels that making Fame was the closest any of her TV assignments have come to live theatre. "There was so much energy and excitement during the

production," she explains. "Every day on the set was like an opening night. That feeling is like food and drink to any actor."

Carol Mayo Jenkins is a winner of the coveted US 'Drama Desk Award', and her roles have taken her from the classics to contemporary drama. She will go, she confesses, anywhere someone will put up a stage.

ALBERT HAGUE PLAYS PROFESSOR SHOROFSKY

Albert Hague is one of the three members of the film cast of *Fame* who have transferred their roles to the small screen. He has had a long and extremely broad career in showbusiness, encompassing the roles of teacher, lecturer, coach and performer, and he has also won a coveted 'Tony' award, and composed hit Broadway numbers.

Born in Berlin, Albert Hague left his homeland because of the political climate, and enrolled at the Royal Conservatory in Rome to pursue his classical music studies. A short time later he was awarded a scholarship at the Cincinnati College of Music in the USA, and arrived there without even the slightest knowledge of the English language.

He graduated from the college as an accomplished composer and pianist — and speaking English!

He was soon a success on Broadway, composing many hits songs for performers such as Burl Ives, working extensively on incidental music for shows, and also composing his own musical, called *Plain and Fancy,* which included perhaps his best-loved song, *Young and Foolish.*

Albert Hague lives in Manhattan with his wife and two children, is actively working, between Fame episodes, on musicals and songs, and is also writing a book, called *Winning Under Pressure.*

And in his spare time…!

PICTURES AT AN EXHIBITION

The silhouette of the dancer arched against the skyline, the trees' autumn severity making a delicate tracery of lines which boldly thrust the leaping figure to the fore.

Another. Two dancers poised like statues in a fountain of leaves. Curiously the wind-driven leaves seemed somehow more alive, almost frantic in their activity when put into frame with this image of solidity that the entwined dancers conveyed.

More. A succession of pictures, kaleidoscoping images of dancers, blurs of colour, black on white starkly contrasted, soft focus visions, superimpositions.

The pile of photographs lay before them on the tablecloth. The background sound of diners, swollen by the undercurrent of dinner table conversation seemed to intrude on Lydia Grant's private thoughts, as the last picture dropped from her hand on top of the others.

"Quite a collection, Mr. Francis."

"Simon."

Lydia nodded amiably. "Simon."

Her companion leaned slightly across the table towards her, restraining his natural eagerness to learn her reactions to his work. His short, wavy brown hair, carefully trimmed, like his moustache, fitted his casual but neat dress, and his quiet almost amused tone completed the picture of a contented, mild man in his mid-thirties. A relaxing, disarming person.

Lydia, relaxed by the food and wine, and disarmed by his likeable manner, had nevertheless retained a keen, critical eye for the portfolio the photographer had promised to show her.

"I'm very impressed by what I see, Simon," she said at last, bringing an instant smile to the other's face. "You obviously have a particular understanding of dance—have you always been so into it?"

"Not always," confessed Simon. "It turned into a big project by itself without my really interfering. I did a series of dance photographs for a magazine one time, a visiting ballet company I think it was, and I kind of developed an interest for it after that."

Simon took a sip from his coffee. "It got so that after a while," he continued, "I found I was developing something of a collection. Now, whenever I can, I take in a show or a rehearsal whichever town I'm working in, add a few more shots to the file. You'd be amazed: I never knew there were that many ways you could dance!"

Lydia smiled. "Having seen some of your stuff, honey, I could no longer be amazed by anything." She stirred her coffee round with the spoon, looking at Simon. "So, all these photographs are going into this exhibition of yours next month?" She raised the cup to her lips.

"That's right," enthused Simon. "I'm staying in New York until then and I figured that a sequence of shots taken at the school would balance the whole thing out." He went of to explain, "I've photographed some of the oldest dance companies in the world, captured the musicals, the big names—"

"And a session with some of our students," interposed Lydia, "would show what's happening with the next generation of dancers?"

"You got it in one!" exclaimed Simon, bubbling with the idea, more animated than he had been

at any time during the evening. "Are you sold on it? Do I hear 'yes'?" He looked meaningfully into her eyes. "Can I bribe you with another coffee?"

Leroy vaulted the swaying form of the girl beneath him, springing forward on his feet as he landed, and moving effortlessly into the irresistible beat that punched through the school lobby, a crowd of onlookers adding to the steady pulse of sound with hand-clapping glee.

His powerful form commanded the stage, visible energy, rapping against his skull and whirling through the air as he fused with the music.

Stepping in from the street Elizabeth Sherwood slowed and noted Leroy's performance. Briefly they caught each other's look, but Leroy spun himself away, wheeling his back on the English teacher. She paused momentarily before disappearing into the office.

The music followed after, but quieter now. Shorofsky was there before her, sifting through the stack of papers that were forever gathering in his pigeon hole.

"They should issue wheelbarrows for this soulless trivia," he said with a gesture of despair. "What are we? Teachers of bureaucrats?"

Miss Sherwood deposited her bags on the counter and went to investigate her own intake. "A heavy load we all must bear," she groaned as she surveyed the assorted stack of forms and memos.

"But why should I want to live my life in triplicate, will someone please tell me?" countered Shorofsky. "Good morning, Miss Sherwood," he continued abruptly, complaint running into greeting without missing a beat. "And how is the world of literature this fine morning? Thriving?"

"Hibernating would be nearer the mark if Leroy Johnson has anything to do with it," she complained, transferring books and papers from one bag to another with some evident but indecipherable purpose.

"How so?" asked Shorofsky, nodding towards the lobby where Leroy was still dancing to the delight of the friendly crowd. "That boy seems to be the last student

round here to be nominated for recluse of the year."

The younger teacher completed her preparations for morning class, and passed her hand over her forehead, pushing her full, long, dark hair away to one side. Shorofsky noted the silence.

"Problems?"

"Leroy's a week late with his book report again. I push him, I give him room—it's all the same, he just puts up barriers all the time," she said directly. "He's developed some kind of automatic reaction, a reflex cut-out, that's triggered by anything that even looks like literature." The warning bell sounded.

Shorofsky gathered the last of his papers together, listening with care. "He needs time, is all."

Miss Sherwood slung one of the bags over her shoulder and brushed herself down to start the day. "If only he weren't so inconsistent," she concluded. "I know he tries sometimes, but getting assignments from him is like trying to force blood from a stone."

Shorofsky chivalrously stood to one side of the door, ushering Miss

Sherwood through. "Hell hath no fury like an English teacher deprived of her book report."

She turned away up the corridor towards the stairs. As she headed for the classroom she found that despite herself her feelings rankled at Shorofsky's jest.

"Leroy Johnson," she said determinedly through clenched teeth, "either you learn to read and write or I'm no teacher!"

The first class of the morning wondered what they had done to deserve such a start to the day.

"One and two and three and...."

Lydia walked along the line of students exercising at the barre, noting each as she passed, offering criticism, advice where needed. "More lift, Julie...that's it...better, better."

The pianist, a late middle-aged lady, a veteran of the business, let her fingers fall gently, regularly over the keyboard, watching the dancers' movements flow with her music, music of the classics, learnt over a lifetime. These youngsters, just beginning.

"One and two and three and...."

Lydia, graceful, watchful, glided the length of the room along the barre, a line of outstretched limbs flexing in a row as she turned to take in the whole class once more.

Leroy stretched, extended, swung his leg forward, balancing on pointed toe, supported by the barre. Never totally at ease with the more classical aspects of dance and movement, he had slowly begun to respond to Lydia's firm but knowing touch.

"A little more arch, Leroy...fine."

The exercise came to a close as Lydia satisfied herself she had touched their limit for the morning. A general breath of temporary relief rustled through the room as the students relaxed muscles, shook out tension, loosened up.

"All right, people. Repeat on the exercise we did yesterday. Two lines. Let's go."

The room buzzed with movement.

"Two lines, I said. Not two lines and a lone reconnaissance scout," Lydia scolded gently. "Get back in line there."

The class settled into the two lines as required, several glances going over to the door as Simon Francis edged his way in, photographic gear over both shoulders.

Mouthing an apology, he moved his way round to the back of the class as Lydia seized the opportunity to introduce him to the students.

"All right, listen, before we move on to the exercise. This is Mr. Simon Francis, who—as you can see—is a photographer." She stood poised before the twin columns of dancers, the light falling on her face, illuminating her olive skin tones so that she glowed. Simon looked appreciatively.

"Mr. Francis," she continued, "will be dropping by over the next day or two to take some pictures of our classes."

Somebody unseen muttered, "Hey! Front page!", and the two lines dissolved in a ripple of giggles. Lydia's voice immediately brought them back in check.

"This is no colour spread for prima donnas," she clipped out sharply. "He's here to capture you children on film. Working. All right? That means one hundred per cent effort; concentrating on what you're doing—and putting your whole body into it. Let's see some heat generated. Remember, this is a routine class—that was the invisible man just walked in here."

Images in space,
a symphony of movement
held motionless in time.
Silhouetted face,
a harmony of colours
in graceful, curving lines.

See me dancing,
Watch me gliding through the air,
See me frozen
in the camera's knowing stare—
See me dancing
See me dancing
Watch me fly

Poetry of hands,
a line of limbs in sequence,
a rippling trail of grace.
Spectacle of dance,
Limbs striving with the effort
Each framed in its own place

See me dancing
Watch me dancing
See me fly.

The classroom stood silent, the seating empty where it had been occupied by an English class moments before. Elizabeth Sherwood sat at her desk, the afternoon's work displayed behind her on the board. A pile of text books and a small sheaf of papers lay about her on the desk. Pens. A notebook. A busy day ending.

"Mr. Johnson?" She spoke quietly, a little wearily, but with some determination. "Is this your book report?"

Leroy leaned back against the front row of desks, his hat set at a studied angle. Cold defiance, a hardness unnatural to an otherwise youthful appearance. Age beyond his years, an adult teenager.

"Well?"

Leroy looked at her, laid back but posed to retaliate if threatened. "Yeah, an' you know it is. An' you got eyes, you can read. I done it. See?"

He stabbed a finger toward the single sheet of paper Miss Sherwood held in her hand. Blank on the back, a little more than half the uppermost side was covered in Leroy's handwriting.

"I've read it," said Miss Sherwood, rather tight-lipped at his immediate flow of aggression. "The question is: have you read the book? It's difficult to tell from this piece of work."

Leroy looked hard at her. "I read it," he said, his voice rising slightly. "An' I done what you asked." He made his statement directly facing his teacher, daring her disagreement, challenging her eyes.

"And you'll do it again," replied Miss Sherwood, equally firm, with an assurance that told Leroy she meant business. "Go away, look at it again, and tell me what you think of it. That's what I asked for, not some re-hash of the stuff on the cover."

"Aw, man," Leroy grated with annoyance. "I have to work nights, swomping out the pool room, an' you know that. I ain't got time to do no assignment again."

Miss Sherwood remained unmoved. "Three things, Mr. Johnson. One: read the book. Two: write the report. Three: have it on my desk first thing Friday." Her penetrating stare brooked no refusal.

The mood that Coco greeted him in the following morning on the steps outside school was as warm as Miss Sherwood's had been chilling. "Hi, Leroy. What's new?"

He vibed into her enthusiasm, felt himself pick up on the stimulus, but kept himself a little in reserve until he could figure what this foxy lady wanted. Coco Hernandez never did anything without a purpose. He'd find out soon enough.

"Nothing much. What's with you honey?" responded Leroy, guardedly. "What's got you so high this morning?"

Coco laughed and linked her arm with Leroy's, walking him into school.

"You and me, hon', are gonna

it by tomorrow morning. Ain't nothing I can do to get out of this one."

Coco's mind turned a wheel or two.

"Leave it to me, Leroy. I know the very man to deliver you the goods. No sweat." She punched Leroy playfully in the arm. "Brother, this is your lucky day."

Later the same afternoon, school out, the corridors rang to the hollow steps of last— minute leavers. In the dance practice room Leroy's ghetto-blaster stood against the wall, instant music locked inside, ready to burst out at the touch of a button.

Leroy and Coco limbered up. In another corner of the room Simon arranged his equipment, checking filters, adjusting lights, watched by Lydia. The room's only other occupant was Danny, insisting he was the sound man, whose presence no one bothered to question once Simon announced he was set.

"Ready when you are, Mr. de Mille," grinned Danny, and released the ghetto-blaster from its electronic cage.

The music, seeping from the machine, slid across the floor, enveloping the two dancers, bringing them to life. An insistent beat sounded in the distance, coming closer, now striding across the room and splitting the dancers apart in a surge of energy.
Simon looked and
shot
and moved and looked and
shot
and shot again
then circled, looking,
shot
a pause, a look, refocused
and shot
as the session powered on. Simon weaved patterns round the dancing figures, a mobile seeing eye, catching moments of beauty, freezing time, suspending actions in a single frame. The energy, agility, its power, the mobility—the film wound on until the thing was done, then all retired, exhausted by their mutual efforts.

be the stars of the exhibition," she triumphed.

"You an' me? What exhibition?"

"The photographer in class this week?"

"Simon whatever-his-name-is. Yeah?"

Coco's eyes twinkled as she bounced along beside Leroy. "He wants me to do a session for him, said I'd to choose a partner. Right?"

Coco stopped and looked at Leroy face to face.

"Right?"

"This partner is me," suggested Leroy. "Am I guessing right so far?"

"On the button, partner. We two birds are gonna be captured in flight and put up on show. Simon says he might even get some pictures placed with the trade papers. How do you like that? Don't say I never use my influence on your career," she added with a smile. "So do you sign me up as your agent now or shall we just play this one by ear? Huh?"

Leroy softened a little round the edges. It sounded fun. "That sounds all right—I'll do it. When's this thing going down?"

"Tonight. Right after school."

Leroy groaned. "I got this book report to do. Miss Sherwood wants

"Let me tell you something, Lydia, Miss Grant," Simon was saying afterwards as he cleared away. "Let me tell you. I've seen dancing magic before—but that girl, she's gonna be something."

Lydia smiled a teacher's smile over the shoulder of the bending man into the mirror. "I know," she said.

"How d'you do that?" asked Leroy. Late Friday afternoon. Home time. "How come Danny Amatullo writes my book report for me?"

Coco smiled knowingly. "You really wanna know? All right. Danny just happens to think Simon is an undercover TY comedy talent scout."

"A what?" Leroy laughed. "You told him that?"

"No, I happened to mention it to Doris. And she told Danny—she sounds so much more convincing than me, and so Danny asked me if I could do him a favour."

"So when he finds out—"

"I only said I thought he might be one. Only a rumour, honey, and my Momma told me never to believe in rumours. Ain't that right?"

The population of the staff room had faded until only Shorofsky remained. Elizabeth Sherwood walked in, surprised to see anyone left.

"I thought everyone had gone," she said.

"We can't go on meeting like this, Miss Sherwood," joked the music teacher. "How was today? Good? Bad?"

"Pass grade. I got Leroy's book report again. A whole page no less, on my desk first thing this morning."

Shorofsky looked impressed. "You obviously talked some sense into him at last."

Miss Sherwood shook her head. "That's what I hoped too, and I was even beginning to think I'd underestimated Leroy…until I realised I'd seen almost the identical piece of work when I marked Danny Amatullo's the other day."

The older teacher shrugged. "It happens. These students here, some of them are so set on succeeding in what they do best they neglect the other delights we offer them here. If Leroy could write like he dances you'd have to clear a cupboard for the paper."

"All I want is a couple of dumb sheets of paper from him, his own thoughts in black in white, that's all."

Shorofsky paused and considered the younger teacher. "Round two to Mr. Johnson, I think. That's defeatist talk."

She looked him squarely in the eye. "Round three coming up. Who said anything about throwing in the towel?"

"Nice of you to drop by."

Simon stood by the open door of the studio and beckoned Lydia in. The room was light and airy, the atmosphere faintly scented. It pleased Lydia as she walked in and surveyed her surroundings.

Simon anticipated her question. "It's on loan to me from a friend while I'm here. He's out of town on an assignment. Can I take your coat?"

Lydia slid off her jacket, which Simon promptly hung on the ornate wooden coatstand by the door.

"Do you have your own studio?"

"A small place in L.A. I see it once in a while, I travel a lot," he explained. "Shall we go through?" He gestured Lydia through a door. "I've put some of the photographs up for you to see before I make the final selection. They're in there."

As Lydia passed through the door she immediately became aware of an entire wall filled, from waist to head height, with photographs. She was unselfconsciously delighted.

Simon moved across to one in particular. "I thought this was the best." Lydia looked. Coco hung motionless in space, suspended, superimposed several times over as she rose and fell, and there was the energy and movement in the supporting figure of Leroy. It captivated her at once.

"Does it have a title?"

Simon shrugged. "Not yet. Do you have any suggestions?"

Lydia thought for a few seconds, looking at the figure, or figures, of Coco as the camera had followed her leap from Leroy's left to right. Like a speed trail.

"I don't know," she mused. "It looks, logically, like several frozen, static moments in time and yet it conveys such a sense of movement. It's almost an optical illusion. Do you know what I mean?"

Simon laughed and leaned against the wall. "I should have you write all my reviews. I wish all my critics were so complimentary."

Lydia turned away from the picture to face him. "You're something of an optical illusion yourself. There one minute, gone the next. Do you never stay still in one place?"

"Me?"

"Other people's studios, borrowed apartments, hotel rooms," Lydia elaborated. "Don't you ever think of stopping some place, every once in a while, just to watch the wheels go round?"

Simon tilted his head toward Lydia and returned her gaze. "Me? No. I'm a moving picture. I just keep right on going." They caught a look in each other's eyes briefly.

Lydia smiled gently. "Pity."

The lobby vibrated to the early morning energy of loud dance music. One or two moved to the sound, but most of the students stood is clusters, cries of delight and "let me see" filtering out from the huddled bodies.

"These are good," said Doris, enthusing as she flipped through the pile of photographs. "Hey, don't crowd me, will you?"

Coco sat with Julie and one or two others going through another sheaf of stills. "Isn't this great, Simon giving us copies of all this stuff," Julie said, as they studied each shot, laughing at some of the expressions they'd been caught with in class.

"Hey, someone just said Miss Grant has given us the okay to do an exhibition of our own with these," added a voice from the back. The idea was greeted with whoops of joy.

"This thing needs organising," Coco stated, sensing an occasion in the making. "A little dancing, some music … let's go see Montgomery."

Julie rose with the others, a look of amusement on her face. "I get the idea that if we all decided to jump off the top of the building together, somehow Montgomery would be invited to organise it."

Coco laughed. "Resident organising genuises are thin on the ground, honey. Montgomery needs all the encouragement he can get—and I give him all the practice he needs."

The girls set off in search of the man in question.

Danny had meanwhile cornered Doris. He was not amused.

"How come you told me this guy was a talent scout, huh? He sent my scripts back, and if that ain't bad enough Miss Sherwood gave me extra English for letting Leroy copy my report."

Doris smiled sweetly. "So next time you don't want me to tell you? Is that it? This time I'm wrong, next time I'm right. You wanna lose your big chance?"

Danny seemed unimpressed.

"Besides," Doris continued, "Leroy had to stay after school and write a whole new book report in front of Miss Sherwood. Three times."

"Three times?"

"I guess she thought it would encourage him to do it right first time round."

Funny how these things turn out, Doris thought to herself. When all's said and done, the only person who didn't lose any points in this game was Coco.

Lydia stood in the office, an envelope in one hand, a mounted photograph in the other. It showed her wistful, delicate, caught unawares by the camera while she had watched Leroy and Coco.

Her cheeks flushed with colour and she turned the portrait over. Neatly written in black ink in the bottom corner was an inscription. *"Next stop Paris.*
People say time passes. They're wrong, it's a fallacy. Time stays constant, it's we who pass through it. Glad to have shared some moments of it with you.
Stay as beautiful.
Simon."

Lydia smiled. Some days you just know are going to go well.

THE BIG APPLE

Every big city has a personality of its own, and New York City simply bubbles with the energy and excitement of its own special magic. New Yorkers love it, and even though it is often violent, often tarnished and often tragic, they still stay loyal to the place they call *The Big Apple*.

Watching American movies and TV programmes you're bound to have heard the names of the five boroughs which go to make up New York City. Their names are Manhattan, the Bronx, Queens, Brooklyn and Richmond. Together they cover an area of about 319 square miles.

Manhattan is the most important borough, and it is here that the tallest skyscrapers stand. It is in fact a little rocky island, and over one and a half million people live here.

Possibly the most famous of all New York's streets is Fifth Avenue, which is lined along all its seven miles with fine shops, hotels and blocks of flats. The world famous theatrical street, Broadway, cuts diagonally across the city, and in the south part is the home of the nation's financial institutions, Wall Street.

To describe New York as a cosmopolitan city would be almost an understatement, as there are people from 60 nations living within its